Teachers As Innovators

An Evaluation of the Motivation of Teachers to use Information and Communications Technologies

Christina Preston Project Director, Director of MirandaNet, Senior Research Associate, the Institute of Education, University of London

Margaret Cox Research Consultant, Professor of IT in Education, King's College London, University of London, Chairperson of the National Association of Co-ordinators and Teachers of IT (ACITT)

Kate Cox Researcher, analyst and report editor, independent consultant

Funded by The Teacher Training Agency, Oracle and Compaq

FOREWORD

As we enter a new millennium, teachers' professional development is becoming widely recognised as an essential process to achieve effective uptake of new technologies in the classroom, along with the necessary equipment and technical support. However, relatively little is known of what motivates teachers to adopt the use of Information and Communications Technologies (ICT) in their teaching. This report of UK teachers' views and motivation is both timely and valuable. The evidence comes from an on-line community of professional practice, MirandaNet, and from other teachers who teach and use ICT in education.

This report comes at a time when the UK government is spending £230 million from the New Opportunities Fund on the training of teachers, with the objective that all teachers will be competent users of ICT by 2002. The parallel initiative of the National Grid for Learning aims to ensure that the whole population can access and communicate via the Internet and associated technologies.

The team brings complementary expertise to this research. Margaret Cox of King's College London has been involved with this research for thirty years, emphasising the need for prolonged training opportunities for teachers. Recently her research has confirmed that ICT motivates pupils, with an exploration of how the learners themselves perceive the value and usefulness of new technology. Margaret Cox is also chairperson of the National Association of Co-ordinators and Teachers of IT (ACITT). Christina Preston of the Institute of Education, University of London, is founder of the first professional on-line community for teachers who wish to develop ICT in education. Over the last six years MirandaNet, and its associated overseas communities, has established a new mode of collaborative professional development supported by commercial organisations and universities. This mode is most appropriate to the evolving learning society. Together with Kate Cox, an MSc graduate in psychology, they have produced this key report for the UK with its extensive investigation into teachers' attitudes towards using ICT and a framework for ICT professional development with teachers.

The findings of this UK study agree with parallel studies in the USA and Australia. The recent study in the USA led by Henry Becker and Margaret Riel[i] focused on a constructivist approach to education and school development with ICT, noting the need for extended professional development opportunities. McDougall and Squires' study[ii], which drew on Australian experiences, also emphasised the layers of professional development in their Framework, the 'Perspective Interactions Paradigm'. In my editorial for the journal in which McDougall and Squires' framework was published, I added, with their agreement, two more foci for teachers' professional development, namely changes in the manager role and evaluation and development of the framework[iii].

I commend careful reading of this report for all those involved in the UK New Opportunities Fund ICT training programmes for teachers. Indeed, all teachers and researchers supporting professional development, including their own, will find value in this report.

Niki Davis

Professor of ICT and Education
Iowa State University Centre for Technology in Learning and Teaching
Marie Curie Research Fellow in Trinity College Dublin
Institute of Education, University of London

---

[i] Becker, H. and Riel, M. (1999). Teacher Professionalism and the Emergence of Constructivist-Compatible Pedagogies. Annual meeting of the American Educational Research Association (AERA), Montreal.

[ii] McDougall, A. and Squires, D. (1997). A framework for reviewing teacher professional development programmes in Information Technology. *Journal of Information Technology for Teacher Education*, 6(2), 115-26. (Available from: www.triangle.co.uk).

[iii] Davis, N. (1997). Framing teacher professional development. *Journal of Information Technology and Teacher Education*, 6(2), Editorial. (Available from: www.triangle.co.uk).

ACKNOWLEDGEMENTS

The project team would like to acknowledge the support for this study given by the Teacher Training Agency, who funded much of the work; Oracle Ltd, who funded further research time, a comparative study in the Czech Republic, the focus group and other meetings, conference presentations and teachers' on-line communications; Compaq Computers, who funded the development of the framework and expert mentoring service, which is presented on their education web site; and the MirandaNet Fellowship, who initiated the project and whose members provided valuable information about their uses of ICT. We are grateful to the members of the National Association for Co-ordinators and Teachers of IT (ACITT) and other educators for participating in the questionnaire survey and attending the focus group meeting. We would also like to thank Francis Howlett (independent consultant) for his work on the training framework, and Professor Niki Davis (Iowa State University) and Professor David Squires (King's College London) for providing valuable comments on the draft report.

CONTENTS

SUMMARY

In the third millennium the widespread use of Information and Communications Technologies (ICT) is impacting on global societies and on education systems. The UK government has responded to this trend by introducing new ICT initiatives, such as the National Grid for Learning and the Computers for Teachers initiative. The New Opportunities Fund has also implemented the ICT training for serving teachers. The aim of the NOF initiative, which began in Spring 1999 and will continue until Spring 2002, is to provide teachers with the opportunity to acquire the necessary knowledge, understanding and skills to become confident and competent in the use of ICT within their subject teaching. However, research has shown that at present many teachers do not yet use ICT in their teaching at all.

This small-scale study investigated how teachers can be helped to integrate ICT effectively into their teaching. We decided to use a sample of teachers who had overcome most barriers and were motivated to use ICT in their teaching on a regular basis to explore the factors that had led to their uptake and sustained use of ICT. In order to obtain such a sample, we sent 135 questionnaires to teachers and other educators who were members of three professional ICT in education associations, namely MirandaNet, National Association of Co-ordinators and Teachers of IT (ACITT), and TeacherNet, and their colleagues who were regular users of ICT including the Internet. These associations provide support for the practices and professional development of teachers using ICT.

Previous action research evidence from the MirandaNet members indicated a number of factors relating to their ability to use ICT in their teaching and in their professional and personal development. Ownership of a personal computer and access to the Internet were already emerging as significant in this mature group of users. Some of this group had been participating in electronic communication for more than six years. Furthermore, some MirandaNet teachers indicated that on-line access provided them with a strong sense of belonging to a 'learning community'. Their case studies concerning their use of ICT revealed more issues that seemed to matter to teachers.

We utilised this information to develop a questionnaire of 203 items to assess those factors that may have an effect on teachers' motivation to use ICT, including their personal ICT use, their attitudes towards using ICT, and the training and support that they have received. However, it is important to note that this is a study of only a small sample of teachers who are experienced ICT users, not an extensive evaluation of all the factors that may affect the use of ICT amongst the whole teaching population.

Using models and theories of attitudes and behaviour in the literature, two components of the technology acceptance model (Davis, Bagozzi and Warshaw, 1989), i.e. the teachers' perceptions concerning the usefulness of ICT and its ease of use, were examined to determine their impact on teachers' use of ICT in their teaching. Using the questionnaire responses and other previous evidence from the members of MirandaNet, the researchers set out to determine those factors that have motivated these teachers to use ICT.

Questionnaires were returned by 82 educators (60.7% of the total of 135 questionnaires that were sent). Almost two-thirds (62.2%) of the sample were males. The sample represented teachers from all the main curriculum subjects. Almost half (47.6%) were IT/ICT teachers or co-ordinators, although only one teacher had been initially trained to teach this subject. The remaining participants were mainly other class teachers or senior managers. 26% worked in the primary sector and 68% in the secondary sector. Challenging the popular assumption that only young teachers have the time and the capacity to manage ICT in the classroom, most of these innovative teachers were senior managers and the majority were also over 40 years old.

Those motivational factors that were found to be relevant to the majority of the teachers were: having access to a computer outside of school and using many different forms of ICT for their personal use; considering ICT to be highly useful, particularly for their teaching and for their pupils; experiencing few difficulties with using ICT; and having attended useful training courses. Although most national governments see their investment in ICT in education as a catalyst for change in teaching and learning, less than half the teachers thought that the ICT courses that they had attended addressed this central issue of teaching style. This would suggest that some courses may not help teachers to adopt those new teaching methods which may be needed to accommodate ICT effectively.

Most of these competent teachers were training others, although they had been to few courses themselves, and half said they did not feel well informed about the National Grid for Learning (NGfL). On the subject of the NGfL, they agreed on the professional value of government web sites, like the Department for Education and Employment, the British Educational and Communications Technology Agency (BECTa), the Virtual Teachers' Centre and the BBC Education web sites which are subject to a government charter. The commercial sites that were visited included newspaper pages and those that relate to music, travel and sport.

Although, many of the teachers felt that they had benefited from the training they had received, they wanted to receive more training and also felt that they needed better resources and more technical support and time to use ICT. In our sample, using ICT more frequently in teaching was associated with finding it easy to think of ways to use ICT in teaching, experiencing fewer difficulties using software/hardware, being satisfied with the resources available, and feeling that using ICT made lessons easier and more interesting. Despite the fact that short special and initial awareness school-based courses were the most popular, longer award bearing courses and working conferences were found to be associated with more frequent use of ICT in teaching.

The findings of our study have many implications concerning the content of training that is necessary to help teachers integrate ICT more effectively into their teaching. It is important to note that teachers value many different forms of training and that the content of training should meet the needs of teachers in accordance with their ICT skills and experience, professional roles, and access to ICT resources. However, in general, the most valued forms of training for the experienced ICT users in our study were ideas for using ICT in the classroom, greater understanding of how ICT helps learning, advanced ICT skills, and discussion with professionals. Inexperienced ICT users may need to learn basic skills as well.

Our findings show that teachers who use ICT in their teaching on a regular basis found ICT relatively easy to use and found ICT to be useful to them, their teaching, and their pupils. Therefore, training programmes to enhance the motivation of inexperienced ICT users should attempt to address teachers' perceptions concerning ease of use and usefulness. Enhancing teachers' perceived ease of use may be achieved by improving their ICT skills, increasing their confidence, and by providing them with adequate resources, sufficient time, and technical and social support. It is even more essential that teachers' perceptions concerning the benefits of ICT are improved. In particular, training programmes should focus on the advantages for pupils' motivation, learning, and interest in lessons. Teachers should also be encouraged to view ICT as making their lessons easier, more interesting and more diverse, and be shown how ICT can improve the presentation of their materials and broaden the content of their lessons. Furthermore, teachers may use ICT more in their lessons if they believe it will give them greater access to computers for their personal use, give them more confidence in using ICT and enhance their career prospects.

It would appear that conventional ICT courses and advisory support were not able to provide all the aspects of ICT training that teachers require. This study offers some insights into the impact of alternative lifelong learning models of ICT training for teachers. One established informal route for teachers is membership of a professional organisation, such as ACITT or MirandaNet. The members of ACITT who participated in our study reported that their organisation had given them greater awareness of the uses of ICT and had enabled them to keep up with advances in ICT. MirandaNet respondents claimed that their membership had provided them with opportunities to meet like-minded individuals in the UK and beyond, to have greater awareness of the uses of ICT, and to keep up with advances in ICT. Half of all the participants in the study said that they would be willing to spend about 15 hours a month tutoring and mentoring colleagues on line, which suggests that these on-line lifelong learning communities have a practical future. Furthermore, some elements of the MirandaNet model, such as long-term mentoring, publishing case studies for peers, industry partnerships in product and service development and professional exchange with teachers world-wide, may be useful to other professional groups who want to set up similar on-line communities.

Overall the findings of this study have contributed to the framework for the professional development of teachers, which is presented at the end of the report. It is a dynamic framework, which is in the process of development, and it will be updated in accordance with new research, educational theories, and responses from teachers and teacher educators. Furthermore, there will be an experimental expert mentoring service organised by MirandaNet Fellows for teachers who want to ask questions about existing practice and explore the potential for similar ICT projects in their own institution (www.mirandanet.ac.uk). The framework has been published on the Internet (www.compaq.co.uk/education) and is therefore available to schools, LEAs, professional associations, and other workers in the field of education.

INTRODUCTION

"It seems foolish to attempt to work on ICT development in isolation when, with a little communication, ideas can be shared, discussed and refined"
Teacher of design and technology and co-ordinator of staff ICT training at a comprehensive school

"(ICT provides) a greater variety of approaches to the same subject area (which) makes it more interesting for me and enables the student to find the style of learning that suits them"
Science teacher at a technology college

"ICT has motivated pupils and given them a real interest in school"
ICT co-ordinator at a comprehensive school

1.1 Research objectives

The objectives of this study were:

1. To identify the types of motivational experiences which teachers have through their use of ICT, the support they receive and the training they have had;
2. To determine the relationship between teachers' motivating experiences and their perceptions about the advantages and disadvantages of using ICT;
3. To identify the most suitable teacher education strategies for increasing motivation;
4. To develop a framework for in-service teacher education, linking teacher education strategies to motivation.

1.2 The rationale for researching teachers' motivation in using ICT

Understanding motivation is the key to understanding human endeavours that succeed against all the odds. In this context, two experienced teacher educators in Information and Communications Technologies (ICT[1]), Bridget Somekh and Niki Davis (1997), recommend that teacher educators engage the intellectual excitement and emotional commitment of teachers as a starting point before addressing the needs of teaching a curriculum. An exploration of motivation can, therefore, offer some insights into the reasons why some worthy and well-funded political initiatives for the integration of computer use into schools have failed to fire most teachers' imagination.

Research into teachers' attitudes, interests, beliefs, and inhibitions in relation to their use of computers may provide answers to a series of questions from teacher educators that relate to teacher motivation. For example, how can we support teachers in becoming more confident, competent and independent learners? What do teachers enjoy most in their use of computers? What activities increase their self-esteem and encourage them to feel comfortable in the use of computers and communication networks? What persuades teachers to commit themselves to complex learning tasks using advanced technologies when their time for professional development is severely limited and under-funded?

[1] When this investigation began, the national curriculum used the term Information Technology (IT) when referring to the subject which was taught, either separately or across the curriculum. The term Information and Communications Technologies (ICT) was used in relation to the use of information and communication devices in other subjects. Therefore, this report uses the term ICT in all cases except when referring to the teaching of new technologies as a subject. However, it is worth noting that the new English national curriculum, published in January 2000, has adopted the use of ICT to refer to its use in other subjects as well as the subject itself.

There have also been many new developments in the field of education that will have an impact on teachers' use of ICT. For example, there is now the added pressure on teachers of parents and students having computers at home. In addition, the growth of the Internet, which has the potential to reduce the barriers of classroom walls and extend the curriculum remit beyond the UK, will provide teachers with many new opportunities. It is likely that these developments will exert additional pressures for change in the classroom. Furthermore, such pressures will impact upon teachers' attitudes towards their professional role and their relationships with other teachers and pupils.

Although there are now new requirements for teachers to use ICT in their lessons, as explained in the next section, evidence from previous research (e.g. Cox and Rhodes, 1990) has shown that teachers using ICT unwillingly or with little conviction of its educational benefits are unlikely to use it appropriately or frequently in their teaching. On the other hand, if teachers are motivated by a belief that ICT will enhance their teaching and their pupils' learning they are more likely to use ICT effectively. Therefore, we believe that it is very important to investigate the motivation of teachers to use ICT.

Some teachers have already overcome many of the barriers associated with using ICT in schools and are sufficiently motivated to use them on a regular basis. The aim of this study was, therefore, to investigate the factors that motivate teachers to use ICT and sustain their use of ICT in teaching. Generalisations from this small and particular study should be treated with caution. However, the results will provide teacher educators, advisors, researchers and staff trainers with evidence relating to the use of ICT in education and the value of on-line learning communities for teachers.

1.3 The context of the study

In this section we consider briefly the context for teachers in the UK regarding social, cultural and political factors which may have an impact on their perceptions of the role of computers in education.

Since 1974 there have been no less than twelve major UK government programmes with an investment of over £250m to support the use of ICT in education. The last fifteen years has been a turbulent period for teacher educators in ICT. For example, in relation to the training of new teachers in ICT, many initial teacher-training institutions had insufficient resources to be able to train their trainee teachers effectively in the use of ICT (Somekh, 1989). Furthermore, the training opportunities for practising teachers were very limited and expensive for schools. Nevertheless, the government was sufficiently confident about the impact of these ICT in education initiatives to begin withdrawing funds from ICT advisory services in 1992. Local Authority advisors indicated concern that this was happening at a time when the introduction of the multimedia computer and the Internet into schools were quickly making familiar hardware like the BBC and the Research Machines' 186 obsolete (Harris and Preston, 1993). In fact, despite all the UK government's initiatives in this period, only a minority of teachers was using ICT regularly in their teaching by 1994/5 (DfEE, 1998a). It would appear, therefore, that the motivation of teachers to overcome the many barriers and difficulties of using ICT may not have been given enough consideration in teacher training programmes.

However, the UK government's support for ICT in education has been growing rapidly in recent years. In 1995, Gillian Shepherd, the Secretary of State for Education at the time, announced a new term "network literacy" (DfEE, 1995). She claimed that "radical changes to teaching and learning styles will become possible in the years ahead as a result of the new communications and information technologies. In facing the challenges we must not forget that education is not just a preparation for working life but a matter of individual, cultural and social development. Quality of life depends on all these factors." The Minister was clearly stating the importance of ICT in education. However, for teachers who were feeling beleaguered by an overload of initiatives, a radical change in their professional practice may have appeared threatening rather than exciting.

In the last five years the changes in education have continued to impinge upon professional practice. The English national curriculum has acknowledged the power of the Internet by changing the subject named Information Technology to ICT, thus emphasising connectivity. The initial framework for the National Grid for Learning (www.ngfl.gov.uk) was launched by the Prime Minister, The Rt. Hon. Tony Blair, on November 6th 1998, with the aim of all schools, colleges, universities and libraries being 'wired' by 2002. The NGfL aims to provide teaching and learning resources, improved access to libraries, museums, schools, colleges and universities and a whole grid of supporting web sites to enable us all to make the most of ICT in education. Over the last 18 months new programmes have been announced which will amount to new funding of over £1.7bn for the National Grid for Learning, ICT training for all teacher trainees and practising teachers, and subsidised computers for teachers who elect to take up this training. The UK government's green paper "Teachers meeting the challenge of change", published in December 1998, emphasises the advantages of ICT for teachers. "The government's major investments in ICT and teaching assistants will make possible effective new combinations of staff and technology to raise standards and extend learning opportunities" (DfEE, 1998b). These opportunities will lead to changes in the classroom whereby "new technology can add new dimensions to lessons, improving both effectiveness and presentation". This paper also suggests that "the use of such technologies extends the scope of teaching by providing information which can be drawn from the World Wide Web by pupils and teachers alike, and (consequently) pupils' capacity to undertake independent research is being dramatically enhanced".

Despite the government's promotion of ICT in education, teachers have had to cope with the government's position that the state cannot afford to provide the resources required for the teaching of ICT in schools. Some schools are looking to industry for resources and financial support, although for some teachers the influence of industry in education is politically unacceptable and may contribute to the negative attitudes about computers that exist in some schools. Nevertheless, public-private partnerships are now important in the establishment of managed services for schools, i.e. industry-provided ICT resources and support (see www.ngfl.gov.uk); and professional development, e.g. the training provider partnerships consisting of collaborations between companies, universities and other training bodies. In addition, there are some positive results concerning industry involvement that may influence teachers' perceptions of the role of the ICT industry in education. For example, Microsoft has set up the Anytime Anywhere Learning Trust to improve access to personal computers and skills training. Oracle is developing an easily accessible web-based learning environment for education professionals with Professor Heppell from Anglia University and a number of Early Adopters from various teaching communities. Tesco has also supported a fleet of ICT advisory teachers and a web site created by children. Furthermore, Compaq are developing education web sites and expert mentoring services with teachers for teachers. With initiatives and inducements such as these it is clear that all teachers will soon be expected to incorporate ICT into their teaching.

1.4 Professional associations involved in the project

In order to investigate the motivation of teachers to use ICT in their teaching this study examined the experiences and attitudes of teachers who were already experienced ICT users. In particular, the members of two professional teacher associations, MirandaNet and ACITT, were targeted. Both these associations provide ongoing help for their members' use of ICT for teaching and learning. Members of a third association, TeacherNet UK, also contributed to our research by completing the questionnaire. This association was set up to provide an on-line service to teachers and other educators, although it was only in the early stages when this study was conducted.

1.4.1 MirandaNet

The MirandaNet Fellowship, which was founded by Christina Preston at the Institute of Education, University of London, with Dr. Harvey Mellar, is a non-profit making international fellowship of teachers, teacher educators, advisors, civil servants, university researchers, librarians, and industry representatives (see Preston, 1999). Scholars, who are recommended by peers as innovative and reflective practitioners, become Fellows when they publish case studies on the MirandaNet web site and mentor their peers. Some Fellows become consultants to industry on product and service development. The MirandaNet community, which has grown from five Fellows in 1992 to just over one hundred, is influenced by the action research approach to ICT teacher education and the emphasis on the management of change in institutions, developed by Somekh and Davis (1997). Growing literature about social interaction and learning on line, particularly about moderation techniques, has also informed the way in which the discussion areas and the web site have been developed (Eisenstad and Vincent, 1998; Jones, 1997; Mason, 1994 & 1998; Rheingold, 1991).

The Fellowship is continually revising its aims to take account of changes in ICT teacher education. Currently the MirandaNet aim, agreed in on-line debate is to "enrich the lifelong learning of professionals involved in education. Using advanced technologies, the Fellowship spans social, vocational, cultural and political divides to help create lifelong learning solutions for education. MirandaNet provides an innovative and inclusive forum for the agents of change that recognises individual learning patterns through peer mentoring and action research strategies. Research, evaluation and on-going discussion underpins and supports good practice and the sharing of enabling strategies. Dissemination and publication are central to the Fellowship process". The cultural impact of ICT on teachers in different countries is a major strand in action research with colleagues in the Czech Republic (Preston, Mannova, and Lengel, 2000). MirandaNet Fellows are also contributing to knowledge about establishing industry-education partnerships (Preston, 2000).

Like most professional organisations, the MirandaNet Fellowship uses conventional means of communication between members and other teachers, such as face to face seminars, conferences, workshops, and meetings as well as mailings, exchange visits, publication in a variety of media and a web site. Reports, case studies and Internet communications have been collected over the years to document the experiences of the MirandaNet members. Some of this evidence, which has contributed to the findings presented in this report, has been the mainstay of the MirandaNet web site, which is a key component for members, introducing teachers and trainers to new styles of teaching and learning. A part-time web editor, funded by industry, ensures that the web site is kept up to date and that teachers get support in publishing their case studies (www.mirandanet.ac.uk). All MirandaNet members also have access to a closed on-line listserv. A monthly ezine (on-line magazine) keeps members up to date with news and resources. The funded opportunity for all the Fellows to develop and evaluate a new free web-based environment, designed jointly by Oracle and Professor Stephen Heppell, has increased Fellows' awareness of the potential of the web for lifelong learning. As a result, an experimental mentoring service for other teachers is now being developed on line (www.compaq.co.uk/education).

1.4.2 National Association for Co-ordinators and Teachers of IT (ACITT)

ACITT was founded in 1987 to support all those working in education for the teaching and use of IT/ICT. Members receive regular newsletters informing them of the latest government developments in ICT in education and a magazine with news articles, features on current issues and practices, and software, hardware and web site reviews. The association also publishes a secondary Informatics curriculum pack (ACITT, 1997) for teaching IT/ICT at Key Stage 3. There is an annual conference at which members can attend keynote speeches and workshops, obtain advice and support from each other and from experts, and get information about the practical uses of ICT in education.

Membership is open to all although the association consists mainly of co-ordinators and teachers of IT/ICT in primary and secondary schools, LEA advisors and inspectors, university academics involved in teacher training and research in IT/ICT in education, and individual consultants. ACITT's advice and opinions are regularly sought from government agencies, schools, LEA personnel, and the media. It is represented on various British Educational and Communications Technology Agency (BECTa) and other agency committees, and has members on working parties developing new curriculum and teaching materials. One of the important functions of ACITT is connecting IT/ICT teachers and co-ordinators, who often feel isolated in their own institutions, providing them with a supportive network of fellow teachers.

1.5 The present study

The present study described in this report was set up to investigate the factors that motivate teachers to use ICT and to sustain their use of ICT in teaching. It was decided that the study should examine the attitudes and experiences of teachers who were already advanced users of ICT in their teaching in order to investigate the factors that had led to their sustained use. The data utilised in this research included evidence collected from such teachers regarding factors that affect ICT uptake. These factors included ease of access at home, training courses attended, perceived benefits of using ICT, perceived usefulness of ICT for administration and personal purposes, and the supportive role of professional organisations. The results of the study are being used to identify models of professional development that are realisable in the current climate based on the models that have been successful in the past and the factors that are identified in this report. Furthermore, based on the findings of this study, guidelines are being developed concerning the professional development of practising teachers to enable them to use ICT appropriately in their teaching and administration and in their own professional development.

The idea for the project came from the authors' experience of two projects: MirandaNet, which is directed by Christina Preston, and the IT and Motivation project, which was conducted by Margaret Cox in order to investigate the effects of IT on the motivation of pupils. The Teacher Training Agency, Oracle Ltd. and Compaq Computers funded the research. A comparative study has also been conducted in the Czech Republic.

1.6 Definitions of motivation

There have been relatively few studies in education that have *focused* on investigating the motivational effects of ICT on teaching and learning. In contrast, in the field of psychology there has been extensive research on motivation. Nevertheless, there is still contention within this discipline concerning the meaning of the term motivation. According to Gross (1992), "trying to define motivation is a little like trying to define psychology itself". More usefully, Miller describes the study of motivation as "the study of all those pushes and prods - biological, social and psychological - that defeat our laziness and move us, either eagerly or reluctantly, to action" (in Gross, 1992). We have utilised aspects of psychological research that are especially relevant to our study. In particular, the theories and models of Fishbein and Ajzen (1975; Ajzen, 1985) and Davis, Bagozzi and Warshaw (1989), which describe the relationship between attitudes and behaviour, have been used as a basis for interpreting some of the influences on teachers' uptake of ICT. Our research has focused on these aspects (which are described in section 2) as they are more directly relevant to the uptake of ICT in education than the many other biological, social and psychological factors referred to in Gross' review of the area.

2 THEORIES OF ATTITUDES AND MOTIVATION

Previous research has identified a number of factors that support or hinder the use of ICT by teachers in the classroom. In order to investigate further the impact of these factors on teachers' ICT use we have utilised Fishbein and Ajzen's theories of attitudes and behaviour (Fishbein and Ajzen, 1975; Ajzen, 1985) and the technology acceptance model developed by Davis, Bagozzi and Warshaw (1989).

2.1 Effects of using ICT on students' motivation

Recent reviews of a range of studies on the impact of ICT on students' motivation, conducted by Cox (1997a, 1999), have identified a number of effects of ICT use relating to motivation. These include enhanced commitment to the learning task, enhanced enjoyment and interest, and increased self-esteem, independence and confidence. There is also evidence indicating that such increases in motivation lead to learning gains (e.g. Ames 1992).

Based on the work of various psychologists on the attitudes and motivation of adults, we have included in our literature review an investigation into what factors have been shown to motivate adults to adopt a range of behaviours, and what can be learnt from these studies about the relationship between teachers' attitudes and their use of ICT in teaching.

2.2 Motivation, attitudes and behaviour

The theory of planned behaviour, based on the theory of reasoned action (Fishbein and Ajzen, 1975), was developed by Ajzen (1985, 1988). According to this theory, shown in Figure 2.1, behaviour is determined by intention to engage in that behaviour. In turn, intention to perform certain behaviours is affected by three factors: attitude towards the behaviour, subjective norm and perceived behavioural control.

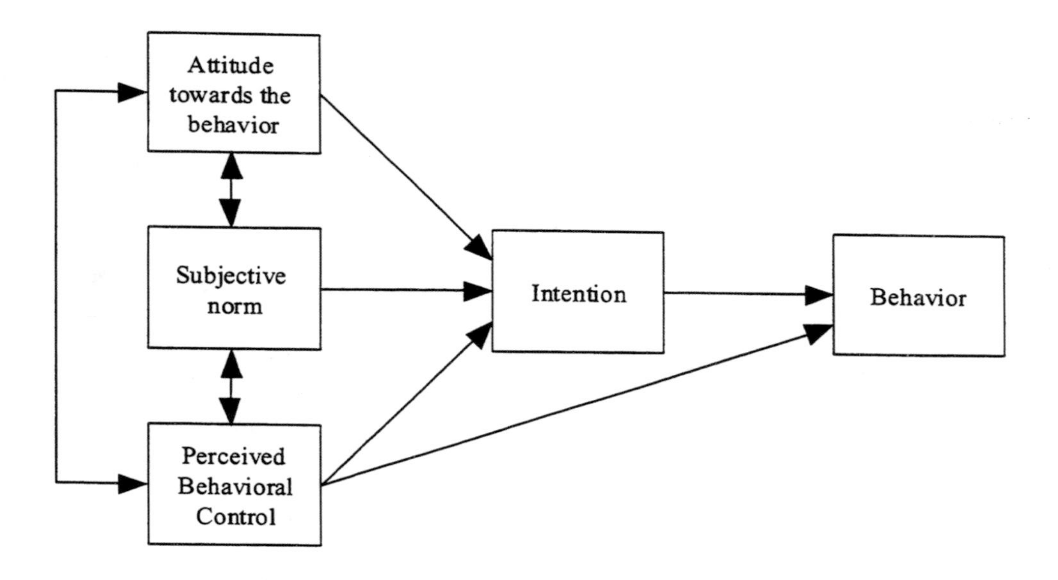

Figure 2.1 - Theory of planned behaviour (Ajzen, 1988, p. 133)

Applying this theory to the motivation of teachers to use ICT, the use of ICT in teaching will depend upon the teachers' *intention* to use ICT. This will, in turn, be influenced by the teachers' *attitudes* towards using ICT in their teaching. In relation to teachers, these attitudes might include perceptions concerning the effects on their role as a teacher, the impact on pupils' motivation, the impact on the teachers' influence in the school, how the behaviour might affect other teachers and so on. Furthermore, we might expect that teachers' attitudes towards using ICT will be influenced by the information they have about the value of ICT, their previous experiences and expertise in using ICT and the expectation that it will contribute to pupils' learning.

The second component included in the theory of planned behaviour, *subjective norm*, represents the perceived social pressures experienced by the individual, i.e. people's beliefs concerning others' attitudes towards the behaviour and the perceived importance of these attitudes. In our case this would be the teachers' perception of the social pressure to use or not use ICT. In particular, they may be influenced by the views of their colleagues, pupils, parents or governors. In many previous studies in other domains, attitudes have proved to be more influential than subjective norms (Ajzen, 1988). However, in the case of using ICT in one's teaching, because of the immense and growing pressures from educational reforms, parents, the media, and so on, it is likely that subjective norm will have a greater impact on teachers' use of ICT.

The *perceived behavioural control* component refers to the extent to which teachers believe themselves to be capable of using ICT in their teaching. This "is assumed to reflect past experience as well as anticipated impediments and obstacles" (Ajzen, 1988, p132). In relation to the use of ICT in teaching, teachers may feel incapable of using ICT for a number of reasons. For example, they may lack confidence in their ICT skills to be able to help pupils in a lesson, they may not be able to adjust their teaching style to accommodate ICT, or they may not know how to use ICT effectively in their subject.

Davis, Bagozzi and Warshaw (1989) developed a "theory of action relating to reasons", the technology acceptance model, based on the work of Fishbein and Ajzen to explain why some people use computers and others don't. According to their model, shown in Figure 2.2, the *perceived usefulness* and *ease of use* of the technology will affect a person's *attitude* towards using it. Furthermore, these factors are influenced by *external variables*. As with Fishbein and Ajzen's model, attitudes affect *intentions* to use ICT, which, in turn, affect *actual use*. The components of Davis, Bagozzi and Warshaw's model are discussed in more detail below. They tested this model with 107 adult users, who had been using a managerial system for 14 weeks. They found that people's computer use was predicted by their intentions to use it and that perceived usefulness was also strongly linked to these intentions.

As this model relates specifically to ICT use and has been shown to be relevant to the uptake of new technologies by adults it was decided that it would be used as a basis for our investigation of the experiences of teachers who use ICT. Using evidence from previous research and the experience of the authors a number of factors were identified that relate to each of the components of this model, which are detailed in the following sections

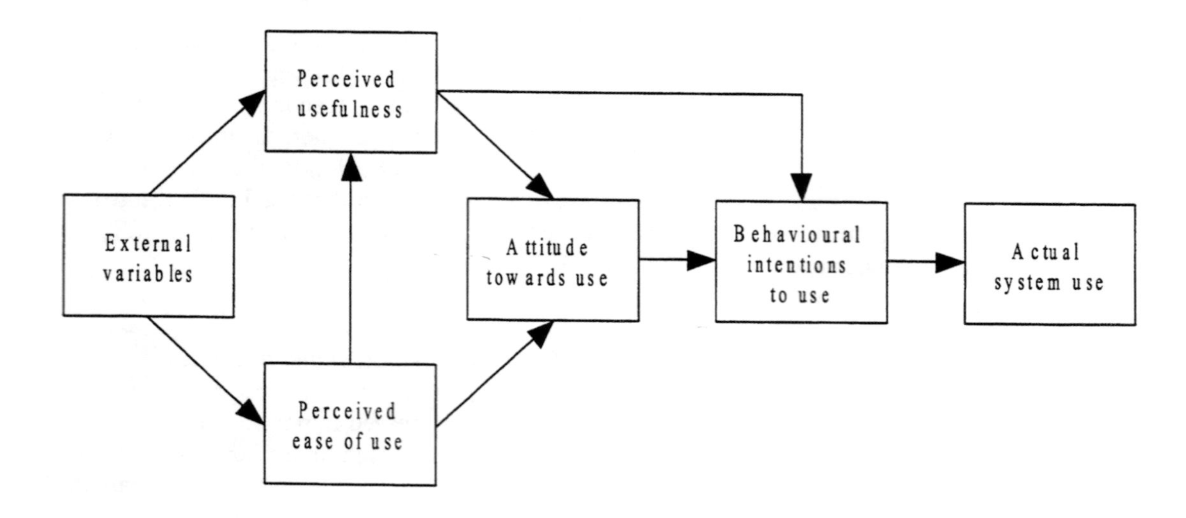

Figure 2.2 – The technology acceptance model (Davis, Bagozzi and Warshaw, 1989)

2.3 External variables

In Davis, Bagozzi and Warshaw's model, the external variables represent the many influences on people that may affect their attitudes and behaviour. Previous research has identified a number of external variables that have an impact on teachers' ICT use. Furthermore, there are other external factors relating to the different government and national policies that have been introduced over many years (see section 1.2), the influence of which has not yet been fully researched. The various external variables that have an effect on teachers' use of ICT include:

- requirements of the national curriculum or national guidelines (Kim, 2000);
- local education authority policies;
- school policies on using ICT (Brummelhuis and Plomp, 1994);
- responsibilities of the teacher (Underwood, 1997);
- training received (Ridgway and Passey, 1991);
- pressure from parents and pupils;
- opinions of colleagues (Kim, 2000);
- membership of professional organisations;
- changes in society, including the rapid growth in the use of the Internet and ICT in general.

It is worth noting that other factors, such as the New Opportunities Fund ICT training for teachers in the UK and the Department of Education and Employment's requirements in the Initial Teacher Training National Curriculum for the use of ICT in subject teaching, may also have a significant impact on teachers' ICT use in the future. Although many of the variables listed above have been identified by a number of research studies as influencing teachers' use of ICT in their teaching (see section 3), only a few could be investigated within the scope of this project. It was decided that our research should examine those factors that can be influenced by teacher educators, senior managers or teachers themselves, such as training, membership of professional organisations and school policies, rather than more resolute influences, such as societal factors or pressure from parents or pupils. Furthermore, it was expected that these other external factors would be reflected in teachers' attitudes to using ICT in their teaching, which were the main focus of our investigation. The attitudes that were examined relate to the perceived usefulness and perceived ease of use components of Davis et al.'s model.

2.4 Perceived ease of use

There are a number of factors that have been identified by previous studies that relate to the perceived ease of use of ICT. The ImpacT Report (Watson, 1993) and other studies have shown that teachers need a wide range of skills and competencies in order to find it easy to use ICT. For example, the ImpacT project showed that teachers found it easier to use educational software if it fitted into their own pedagogical practices (Watson, 1993). In addition, the teachers participating in the Jasper project found it easy to use ICT software when they were provided with a supporting network of teacher colleagues (The Cognition and Technology Group, 1997). Gardner and his colleagues (1993) found that teachers could use laptop computers when given sufficient training and support. The factors identified by previous research relating to perceived ease of use of ICT include:

- ability to use software/hardware;
- confidence in using ICT;
- ability to control the class;
- ability to think of new lesson ideas;
- perceived impact on the content of lessons;
- adequate training and support;
- being supported by colleagues.

2.5 Perceived usefulness

If teachers perceive ICT to be useful to them, their teaching and their pupils' learning, then according to the evidence of previous studies (see Cox, Preston and Cox, 1999) they are more likely to have a positive attitude to the use of ICT in the classroom. In our review of the literature we identified a number of factors which relate to teachers' perceived usefulness of ICT:

- whether or not the lessons are made more interesting, enjoyable, or diverse for the teacher;
- whether or not the lessons are made more difficult for the teacher;
- impact on the presentation of materials for lessons;
- impact on pupils' motivation and learning;
- perceived contribution to administrative tasks;
- impact on the teacher's confidence;
- impact on the teacher's prestige;
- perceived effect on career prospects.

Teachers' attitudes relating to many of these usefulness factors will depend upon how easy they perceive using ICT to be, both for personal use and for use in teaching.

According to Davis, Bagozzi and Warshaw's model (1989), the greater the perceived usefulness and perceived ease of use are, the more positive the attitudes of teachers will be to the use of ICT and consequently, the more likely they will be to use ICT in their teaching. One major aim of our research project was to investigate the relevance of this model for experienced ICT teachers, and to determine which factors they felt were important.

3 EVIDENCE FROM PREVIOUS RESEARCH

In the previous section we have detailed a range of factors that may contribute towards the uptake of ICT by teachers, relating to teachers' individual beliefs and attitudes and more general external influences. The motivational effects that have been identified from the studies of attitudes to new technologies include enhanced commitment to the learning task, enhanced enjoyment and interest, and increased self-esteem, independence and confidence. People have been found to acquire a positive attitude to new technologies if they perceive them to be useful and easy to use (Davis, Bagozzi and Warshaw, 1989).

There has been a range of studies of the perceived social pressures that also have an impact on teachers' motivation to use ICT, such as the requirements of the national curriculum, and pressures from parents, pupils, and the media. Some of the evidence relating to developing positive attitudes amongst teachers and the influence of external factors is presented in this section, although this is only a small selection of the wide range of research studies which now contribute to this field.

3.1 The importance of teachers' attitudes for the uptake of ICT

Many studies have demonstrated the influence of teachers' (and other adults') attitudes towards adopting new technologies on the use of these innovations. A study by Brummelhuis and Plomp (1994) shows the importance of a range of variables relating to individual teachers for the uptake of ICT in schools. They studied the effects of several national programmes funded by the Dutch government for the introduction of computers in primary and secondary schools, including the relative importance of individual teachers and the school policy. They concluded that the teachers' computer usage very much depended upon variables relating to the individual teachers themselves rather than on school policy.

In another study by Philips et al. (1999) of 60 teachers in the UK using laptop computers, the researchers found that the majority showed enhanced positive attitudes through increased interest, commitment and enjoyment and that there was a resultant significant increase in their use of ICT. In contrast, the small minority of seven teachers who used the laptops infrequently "appeared to lack commitment in practice,...have a rather passive approach...and look for reasons for not doing things".

Brummelhuis and Tuijnman (1992) also demonstrated that attitudes relating to teachers' perceived confidence in using ICT had a direct influence on the uptake of ICT by German teachers. Furthermore, research by Gardner et al. (1993) showed that negative attitudes, particularly those relating to computer anxiety, were a major barrier to the use of ICT by individual teachers. Case studies of teachers' use of the Internet for on-line professional development have shown that a supporting network of colleagues helps to sustain the use of ICT in the individual teacher's subject (Preston, 1999). Other evidence demonstrating the importance of attitudes for the use of ICT in teaching has come from studies comparing users and non-users of ICT.

3.2 Studies comparing users and non-users of ICT

Karahanna and Straub (1999) conducted a large-scale survey of the sequence of activities that led to the initial adoption and subsequent continued usage of Windows by employees in a large financial institution in the United States. They examined how adoption/usage is influenced by individuals' beliefs. Two groups of adults were selected for the study: those already using ICT and potential ICT users. The researchers investigated whether there was a difference between the relative importance of attitudes and subjective norm (see section 2.2) in determining Windows use by potential adopters and by existing users. In addition, they examined whether the participants' behavioural beliefs (i.e. beliefs about using ICT) and normative beliefs (i.e. beliefs about other people's opinions regarding ICT use) changed when they adopted ICT.

The results from Karahanna and Straub's study of a final sample of 107 potential adopters and 161 existing users of Windows showed that the only significant reason for potential adopters to use Windows was the social environment, e.g. peer group and management pressure. In contrast, the users were mostly influenced by their voluntariness (i.e. the degree to which they perceived their adoption and use of ICT to be voluntary) and their attitude towards the technology itself. According to the researchers, this "may suggest that social pressure from the organisation environment may be an effective mechanism to overcome adopter initial inertia in adopting IT. Even though this effect vanishes following adoption, use of social norms may be important in inducing initial use and the subsequent development of perceptions".

They also found that for potential adopters the most important attitudes were: perceived usefulness, ease of use, the extent to which the results of using Windows were observable and communicable to others, and visibility, i.e. the degree to which the innovation is visible to others within the organisation. In contrast, the most important attitudes for the users were found to be perceived usefulness and the perceived effect of using ICT on image or status in the working environment.

The social environment for potential adopters was also found to be important for secondary school teachers in a study by Kim (2000). He investigated the main reasons for 121 teachers for using or not using ICT in their teaching. For the potential adopters (non-users) the most important reasons for not using computers were found to be lack of confidence in using computers and lack of knowledge and skills in using them in teaching. For the users the most important reasons given for not using them more frequently were insufficient numbers of computers, lack of time to learn a new program and difficulty in booking the IT room. Kim also found that an important factor leading to intention to use ICT was a sense of obligation caused by the social environment and various external factors.

These findings suggest that teachers may be motivated to adopt ICT in their teaching by improving their confidence, knowledge and skills in using ICT and by changing their attitudes concerning the perceived usefulness and ease of use of ICT. In addition, this research has shown that teachers' use of ICT is influenced by peer group and management pressure, although clearly, it would be more desirable for teachers to use ICT because they want to not because they feel obliged to. Furthermore, these studies imply that teachers' continued use of ICT would be increased by enhancing their perceptions of the usefulness of ICT, its effect on their status within their school, and the accessibility of ICT resources.

3.3 The influence of external factors

The findings discussed above demonstrate the impact of teachers' attitudes towards ICT on their adoption of ICT within the classroom. However, Kim's and others' research has shown that there are many external factors that can have a major influence on teachers, enabling them to develop from being a potential adopter to a regular user.

During the early days of the introduction of computers into schools many educators believed that the principal factor that would enable teachers to use ICT was the 'adequate' provision of ICT resources (software and hardware). Since 1985 the Department for Education and Employment has conducted large scale surveys of English and Welsh schools every two years to assess the level of ICT resources and the use of ICT within all curriculum areas. These surveys showed that between 1985 and 1992 the number of computers in schools had increased by nearly 400% and since 1992 there have been continuing increases in levels of resources.

Many people expected that this large increase in ICT resources would lead to a large increase in the number of teachers using ICT, yet the most recent government survey of ICT in schools (DfEE, 1998b), which was based on questionnaire returns from 977 secondary and 938 primary schools, suggests that this is not the case. Although there were found to be over 3124 primary and 2965 secondary schools connected to the Internet, only 7% of science teachers, 8% of mathematics teachers, 6% of foreign language teachers and 10% of English teachers reported making substantial use of ICT in their subject teaching. The ImpacT study (Watson, 1993) showed that there was a minimum level of ICT resources required for teachers to be able to incorporate ICT into their teaching. However, this research also showed that teachers in some schools with a low level of resources used ICT much more than teachers in some other schools with more resources. These findings suggest that although level of resources is an important factor, providing teachers with ICT equipment is not sufficient for enabling them to use it in their teaching.

An earlier international study of the use of computers in 22 education systems was carried out by the International Association for the Evaluation of Educational Achievement (IEA, Pelgrum and Plomp, 1991). Amongst many other issues, school principals (head teachers) were asked their reasons for not using computers in schools. Table 3.1 shows, for each of the five participating countries, the percentage of school principals that gave each of the most common reasons. These findings showed that four of the seven most commonly reported reasons were external factors, relating to the accessibility and adequacy of resources and financial support.

Table 3.1 – The percentage of school principals, from five different countries, who gave each of the most common reasons for not using computers

Reasons	**Belgium**	**Greece**	**Japan**	**Portugal**	**Switz.**
Insufficient computers	34	49	21	31	34
Insufficient software	14	16	11	11	5
Teachers lack knowledge	49	52	63	42	54
Insufficient time	42	25	7	10	18
Difficult computer location	24	31	12	22	26
Insufficient training	9	39	56	43	6
Inadequate financial support	38	36	57	80	26

One of the external factors shown by the IEA study to affect ICT use, insufficient training, has been found by many other more recent studies to be one of the most influential barriers to teachers using ICT on a regular basis (Cox, 1997b). The need for substantial training was also identified in an earlier longitudinal research project into the uptake of computers in primary schools from 1985 to 1989, which was conducted by Cox and Rhodes (1990). They showed that, even for teachers who had followed several courses and who had regular local educational authority support, the uptake of computers in primary schools was limited to a small minority of teachers. Fewer than 10% of the teachers were using computers on a regular basis, even after having computers in their schools for four years. A major finding from this research was that teachers needed to have long-term substantial training if they were to integrate ICT regularly into their teaching. This finding was substantiated by the ImpacT study (Watson, 1993), which found that, apart from ICT teachers, teachers who had not had substantial training in the use of ICT were unlikely to use it regularly in their teaching. Although these studies were conducted some time ago, similar findings have been reported by Underwood (1997) in a more recent investigation into the effects of teacher training on teachers' ICT use in schools. The importance of teachers' professional development to the uptake of ICT in their teaching is discussed further in the following section.

3.4 Professional Development

Numerous research studies have found training, and professional development in general, to be crucial to the successful uptake of ICT. Training has been provided for the use of ICT in teaching ever since the early introduction of computers into schools, but has not yet had the desired effect in terms of producing widespread use of ICT by teachers. It is discussed briefly here to reveal some of the issues that are relevant to teachers being motivated to use ICT.

3.4.1 Previous training programmes

During the 1970s and 1980s most training programmes were based on the underlying assumption that teachers only needed to be taught how to use the technology in order for them to be motivated to use it in their teaching; rather like training teachers how to use a video player and then expecting them to use it in their lessons. One example was a national programme in the UK, launched in the early 1980s, for ICT in teaching and learning in schools, the Microelectronics Education Programme ('MEP', from 1982-1986), which included a national scheme for the training of teachers. This programme utilised a cascade and escalation approach, whereby some teachers attended a short course (from 6-20 hours) to receive training about ICT and were then given the task of taking their new found knowledge and skills back into the schools to train their colleagues. It was assumed that with sufficient training teachers would be motivated to use computers in their teaching.

Research has shown that approaches such as these are not sufficient to induce sustained use of ICT in teaching. For example, studies by Bliss et al. (1988) and Cox et al. (1988) showed that even the substantial training of one or two teachers, involving several evenings per term, did not lead to a change in their practice nor the sustained uptake by the other teachers in the school. These and other research projects over the last 20 years have shown that such national and local innovation projects have been less effective than hoped, with only a minority of teachers being motivated to use ICT regularly in their teaching. Previous research suggests that these courses may not have succeeded because they did not address the teachers' understanding of the need for change in professional practice.

3.4.2 Understanding the need for change in professional practice

Research studies (Cox et al., 1988, Cox, 1994) have shown that the majority of short courses to train teachers in the uses of ICT offered in the UK in the 1980s and early 1990s focused on the technical aspects of ICT with little training about the changes in pedagogical practices required or how to incorporate ICT into the curriculum. This means that after teachers had attended short courses such as these they still did not know how to use ICT for teaching pupils, they only knew how to run certain software packages, how to format disks, or how to print documents. There were many such courses offered all round the UK that had very little long-term impact on the uptake of ICT in schools.

Fullan's (1991) evaluation of projects to promote educational changes in America, Canada and the UK showed that one of the most fundamental problems in education reform is that people do not have a clear and coherent sense of the reasons for educational change, what it is or how to proceed. He maintains that teachers who resist change do not deny the need for change, but rather are unable to bring about the changes necessary. He argues that teachers who resist change are often those who are expected to lead developments and therefore only resist change because they lack the necessary education in the management of change and are given insufficient long-term opportunities to make sense of the new technologies for themselves.

There are also many studies that have shown that once teachers have finished their initial training they do not expect to need much further training and therefore do not take the initiative to improve their practice and learn new skills. According to Underwood (1997), they are "not given to questioning their professional practice". Feiman-Nemser & Buchanan (in Desforges, 1995) claim that "many teachers are perfectly well satisfied with their practices and are unlikely to question prevailing educational processes". Furthermore, Desforges argues that, in order for teachers to make changes to their professional practice, "a considerable effort is necessary to create the possibilities of restructuring knowledge (about teaching and learning) in the face of experience". He also maintains that "in regard to old knowledge we can speculate that the impact of new experience (e.g. using ICT) will be severely attenuated if it is in conflict with teachers' basic ontological categories, e.g. their beliefs about the nature of their job or the nature of childhood". Teachers need to be encouraged to adopt new teaching methods and to incorporate developments of theories of learning into their teaching. If teachers see no need to change or question their current professional practice they may not take-up the use of ICT in their teaching or change the way in which they use ICT as the technology develops.

3.4.3 Successful innovation strategies

In spite of the problems discussed above, some positive things have been learnt from previous initiatives and training programmes. Research by Fullan (1991) has shown that the most effective way to bring about the adoption of an innovation in a school is to engage the whole school in a democratic process of planning change. This means that all the teachers are involved in the decision to adopt ICT in the school and are supportive of any individual teacher going on a course and are willing to learn from their new knowledge and skills when they return. If members of the school, and the head teacher in particular, are not committed to adopting change and the introduction of ICT, then if one teacher goes on a course, the rest of the school sets up antibodies to any new ideas that are brought back into the school. The last thing the other teachers will then do is to change their practice.

Goldstein (1997), a senior UK OFSTED inspector, reporting on the variable quality and extent of ICT use in schools, identified the need to improve teachers' ICT confidence and develop their self-esteem. He recommended the development of pedagogical practices for teaching ICT to enable teachers to adopt it more readily in their teaching, and to build on good traditional practices for teaching other subjects. Most importantly, he recommended the strengthening of networks and training facilities for teachers that disseminate good practice.

Longer training courses, spread over a year, enable teachers to have the time to practice in between sessions back in their schools and to assimilate enough expertise and knowledge to be able to continue to use them within their curriculum (Cox, Rhodes & Hall, 1988). In addition, projects in which individual teachers have been given portable computers to develop their own personal ICT skills have shown that teachers then start to use them in their teaching as well (Stradling et al., 1994). Other studies of teachers' professional development have shown the beneficial effects of teachers feeling part of a wider community involved in educational change.

3.4.4 Learning communities

The research into the effectiveness of teacher training discussed above has shown that when teachers experience training in isolation from their work colleagues and from their institution it is often difficult to adopt new techniques and methods once the training has ended. Previous studies have also shown that for teachers to become effective ICT users they need continuing support and encouragement from their colleagues (Underwood, 1997). One way of achieving this is to enable teachers to be part of a learning community with professional development being a core aim.

Evidence from members of the MirandaNet project has shown that learning communities can foster positive attitudes towards using ICT (Preston, 1999). Reports from the teachers that belong to this learning community have shown that the support enables them to use ICT in their teaching even if few other teachers in their schools are doing so. MirandaNet fellows have reported many benefits of being part of a learning community for their professional practice. The most important of these are "on-line links preventing professional isolation, international focus on good classroom practice, peer mentoring gains, and peer support advantages" (ibid. p. 221).

The Jasper Project (The Cognition and Technology Group, 1997) in the United States, which involved hundreds of teachers using 12 video-based disk adventures, found that teachers were motivated to sustain their use of the ICT by considering themselves as learners and by being part of a sharing community of educators. "Problem based curricula, such as Jasper, provide teachers with a shared context that they can refer back to as they discuss their own attempts to change their teaching and assessment practices". This project identified a number of advantages of learning communities of teachers: anchored collaboration around problems and projects, collaboration and distributed expertise, intrinsic and extrinsic motivation, connectedness to a broader community of audiences, frequent opportunities for formative self assessment, the use of (shared) tools to work smart, and support for the technology.

"Central to the development of professional learning communities are the attitudes people have about what it means to be a successful member. People...become better able to learn when they move from a model of expert to a model of accomplished novice... If they want to participate in a learning community ... they must learn to value the wisdom of practice that teachers bring to the community. In our experience, this wisdom of practice represents a body of knowledge that is extremely valuable and important to learn" (ibid. p.125).

3.5 Summary and implications

The evidence discussed in this section has demonstrated the influence of training and other external factors and variables relating to individual teachers, such as their attitudes, knowledge and skills. The studies comparing non-users and users of ICT have shown that, for potential adopters (non-users), the most important factors are the social environment, knowledge and skills in ICT use, and attitudes, such as perceived usefulness, ease of use and confidence. For users, the most important factors promoting sustained use are positive attitudes towards the technology, the time and resources available, and voluntariness. The lack of efficacy of past training programmes shows the need for more comprehensive professional development for teachers, which addresses factors such as attitudes and confidence, the need for changes in pedagogy and for ongoing professional development in line with advances in technology and educational theories, and the support of others. Effective elements of professional development approaches include involving the whole school in changing practice, the development of teachers' personal ICT use, longer training courses and the development of learning communities.

If professional development programmes and the New Opportunities Fund training are to be effective, further investigation into what motivates teachers to use ICT in their teaching is needed. The aim of this study was to find out whether there are particular attitudes and motivational factors that can be promoted and supported to help the non-users become users and to integrate ICT effectively into their teaching.

4 THE STUDY

Informal relevant research for this project began in 1992 with the collection of the reports from the MirandaNet members. This was followed by the commissioned study, beginning in May 1998 and ending with a focus group meeting in March 1999, with the analysis of all the data being completed by November 1999.

4.1 Research objectives

The objectives of the whole study were:

1. To identify the types of motivational experiences which teachers have through their use of ICT, the support they receive and the training they have had;
2. To determine the relationship between teachers' motivating experiences and their perceptions about the advantages and disadvantages of using ICT;
3. To identify the most suitable teacher education strategies for increasing motivation;
4. To develop a framework for in-service teacher education, linking teacher education strategies to motivation.

4.2 Project methodology

In order to investigate the factors that enable teachers to use ICT in their teaching we examined the psychology literature to identify suitable theoretical models which could be used as a foundation for selecting factors that might influence teachers' motivation to use ICT. We explored those influences on teachers who were experienced ICT users. We planned to collect evidence from teachers who had been using a range of ICT resources in their teaching for some time and had shown evidence of a commitment to using ICT by either being a member of a teacher organisation associated with ICT or a colleague known to be an experienced user. Therefore, a sample of teachers, who were unrepresentative of teachers as a whole, was utilised in order to investigate those factors that led to the advanced use of ICT in teaching. The project was conducted in four main stages.

Stage 1 – Literature search and examination of MirandaNet information
Stage 1 involved:

- The analysis of a range of paper based and electronically based evidence collected from MirandaNet scholars and fellows, who have been providing written reports of their uses of ICT and have attended seminars and conferences to discuss their work. This work has been documented in the form of reports, published articles and individual e-mail communications.
- An on-going literature review of other research publications, and practical accounts of the motivation of teachers to use ICT and other relevant factors relating to teachers' uptake of ICT in their teaching.

Stage 2 – Questionnaire survey
A questionnaire (see Appendix B) was designed to collect evidence from teachers and other educators, who were experienced users of ICT, about their ICT experiences, expertise and use in teaching, and their attitudes towards the value of ICT for teaching and learning, the training they had received and, when relevant, their attitude towards being a member of an association. The main sections in the questionnaire are shown in Table 4.1 below.

Table 4.1 - Main sections of the research questionnaire

Section	Title of section	Type of information requested	Number of items
1	Personal information	Name, age, teaching commitments, subjects taught	16
2	Personal use of computers	Ownership, type of computer, ICT skills, ICT uses, Internet uses	24
3	Use of computers in school/institution	Number of years used, types of use, frequency of use, professional web sites valued	23
4	Using ICT in teaching	Value and difficulties of using ICT, advantages and disadvantages of using ICT	33
5	Using the Internet in teaching	Number of staff and pupils with e-mail addresses, Internet services, NGfL issues, purpose of using the Internet	48
6	Professional development	Types of courses attended, other support received, benefits of in-service training, contribution to the professional development of others	25
7	Using ICT for administration	Types of ICT use, responsibility for task	9
8	Professional association information	Length of membership, perceived value of the services available, factors limiting the usefulness of membership	25
		Total number of items	**203**

The sample who were sent the questionnaire consisted of:

- 15 members of MirandaNet, with an extra two each to give to their colleagues who were regular ICT users (total 45);
- 15 members of the National Association for Co-ordinators and Teachers of IT (ACITT), with an extra two each to give to their ICT using colleagues (total 45);
- 15 members of TeacherNet UK with an extra two each to give to their ICT using colleagues (total 45). TeacherNet members were targeted, along with ACITT and MirandaNet members, as they exemplify teachers who want to be part of an Internet community and have an e-mail address, and consequently are relatively advanced users of ICT.

Stage 3 –Developing a framework for INSET strategies to motivate teachers
This stage involved identifying the main issues relating to the needs of all teachers and also the needs of teachers as individuals. We considered a number of variables that distinguish between teachers that may influence the kind of training they should receive. These variables included their roles and responsibilities within their school, their ICT expertise and experience and the level of resources available.

Stage 4 –Focus group meeting
A focus group meeting was held with twenty educators to consider the issues revealed during stages 1, 2 and 3 of the project in order to assess teachers' (and other educators') views on the findings and the dissemination of our results to others (see introduction to the professional development framework).

4.3 Source materials

We conducted a review of the materials collected by MirandaNet, and relevant academic and professional journals. These materials included:

- MirandaNet case material published on the Web and in newspapers;
- transcripts of e-mails between MirandaNet members;
- files submitted by each MirandaNet scholar;
- articles from academic and professional journals;
- newspaper articles;
- Web government documents – e.g. from TTA, BECTa, QCA;
- other academic and relevant papers on the Web.

4.4 Research evaluation strategies

The research evaluation strategies involved:

a. Analyses of the MirandaNet data and evidence from the literature.
b. A questionnaire survey. (The questionnaire was reviewed and piloted by 10 peers from four different associations and was revised in the light of their feedback).
c. Analyses of the results in terms of their relevance to teachers' attitudes, ICT use in their teaching and their professional development. The focus group of 20 teachers and other educators, many of whom also responded to the questionnaire, was used to review the results and contribute to more detailed explanations relating to the specific responses to the questionnaire and other data. The participants were mainly members of MirandaNet, ACITT, and TeacherNet, with representatives from the Teacher Training Agency and OFSTED and education specialists from universities.

5 RESULTS

This section details the findings of the analysis of the questionnaire responses and existing MirandaNet material that was relevant to the focus of this study. The results from the questionnaire have been analysed using SPSS (a statistical package for social sciences) and the spreadsheet package Excel. Further results about specific factors regarding the uptake of ICT in teaching are discussed in Cox, Preston and Cox (1999).

When this study was conducted, Information Technology (IT) was the official term for both the subject itself and the use of technologies in other subjects. However, as explained at the beginning of the questionnaire (see Appendix B), the new term ICT, i.e. Information and Communications Technologies, was becoming more widely used in the field of education. This was to recognise the growing use of communication technologies, such as the Internet, e-mail, video conferencing etc., in education. In the questionnaire, items about existing uses in the curriculum referred to the term IT, whereas items concerning personal use, future use, and training referred to the term ICT, anticipating a more extensive use of the communication elements of the technology in these areas than within teachers' everyday lessons. Although the new English national curriculum (QCA 2000) has now adopted the term ICT for the subject as well as the use of new technologies in all subjects, the terms are often used interchangeably by many people in education. However, due to the wide adoption of the term ICT, we have simplified the discussion of our findings by using this term in all cases except for the teaching of the subject itself.

5.1 Description of the questionnaire sample

Questionnaires were returned by 82 educators; 60.7% of the total of 135 questionnaires that were sent. 51 (62.2%) males and 31 (37.8%) females responded. The higher proportion of males in the sample may be due to the greater number of male IT teachers and co-ordinators that exist nationally. The distribution of ages of the questionnaire sample, shown in Figure 5.1, indicates that the majority was in the middle-aged bracket. However, as many of the secondary school respondents in our sample held senior positions in their own departments, e.g. as ICT co-ordinator (see Figure 5.4), one would expect that they would have several years teaching experience already and therefore be older than the majority of newly qualified teachers.

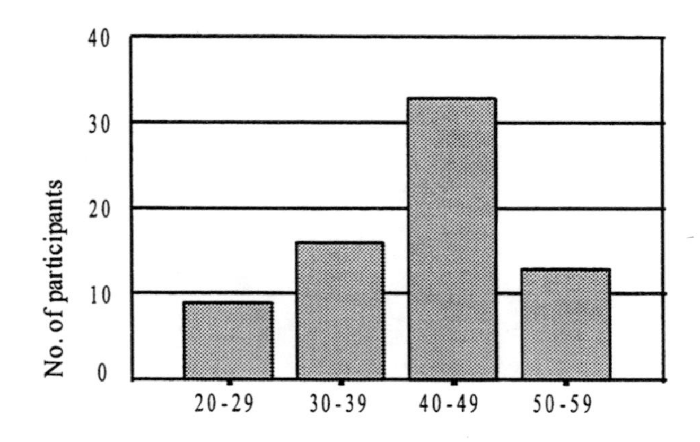

Figure 5.1 - Age distribution of the sample

The majority of the respondents were not members of the professional organisations that were targeted for this project. Although, 37 respondents were from the three associations, namely MirandaNet, ACITT, and TeacherNet (82% returned), the remaining 45 were their colleagues (50% returned). The distribution of the respondents' membership of these associations is shown in Figure 5.2.

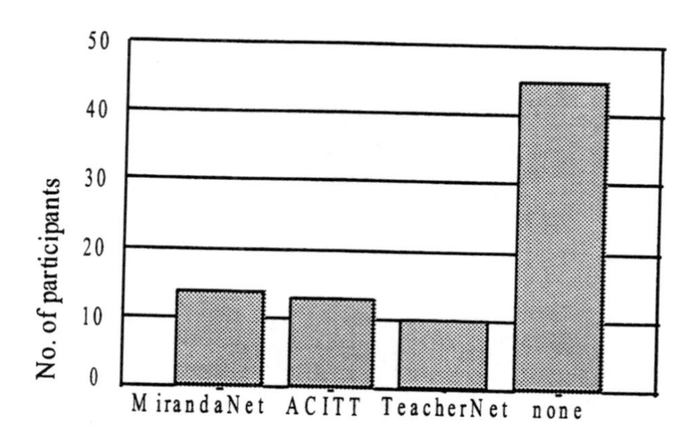

Figure 5.2 – Respondents' membership of the ICT in education associations

Figure 5.3 shows the distribution of the phases in which the respondents teach. The majority were teachers in secondary schools, with just over a quarter from primary schools. A very small minority stated that they teach in the 6th form or are involved in cross phase work. Some of the respondents were teacher educators or held other positions outside of schools. Figure 5.4 shows the job distribution of the respondents, indicating that the largest group were ICT co-ordinators (43.9%), with a small number of other IT teachers (3.7%), 24.4% being other subject teachers, and 23.2% being senior managers. The remainder (under 10%) were in a range of other educational positions, such as librarians, special needs teachers and IT technicians. However, it is worth noting that a number of participants fell into more than one category of employment. For example, some of the senior managers were also the ICT co-ordinators for their institutions. The teaching responsibilities of the questionnaire respondents varied from no teaching responsibilities at all for non-teaching staff, such as IT technicians, to 25 hours a week or more for class teachers. Most of the senior managers had some teaching responsibilities and many of the ICT co-ordinators taught other subjects, including psychology, physics, and mathematics, as well as teaching IT.

The management responsibilities varied greatly amongst the sample. A few of the questionnaire respondents reported that they had no management responsibilities. However, the majority of the sample, and in particular the senior managers and head teachers, had some responsibilities, including staff training, curriculum delivery, developing school policy, and time-tabling.

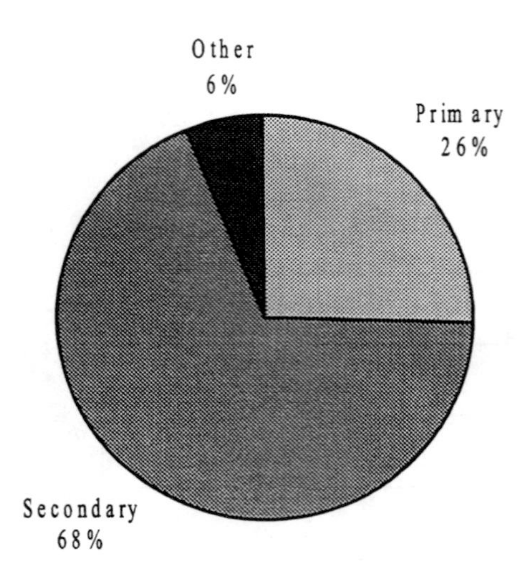

Figure 5.3 - Distribution of respondents by education sector

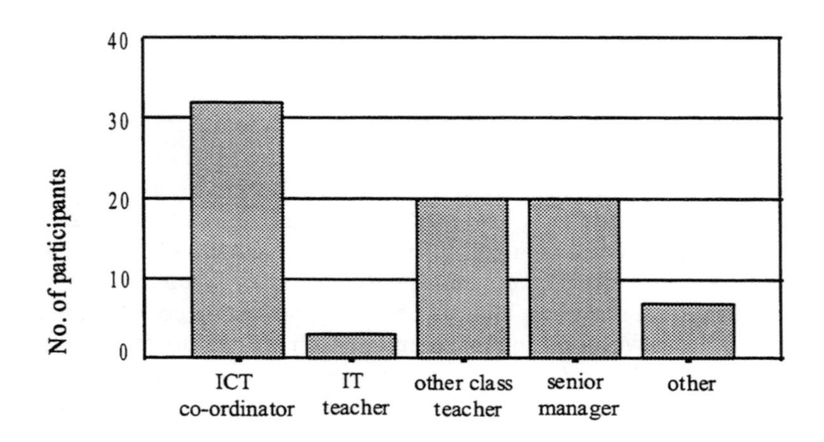

Figure 5.4 - Employment of the respondents

Just under three-quarters (74.4%) of the questionnaire participants reported that they were obliged to teach IT. Some of those who said they were not obliged to teach IT did not have any teaching responsibilities. Figure 5.5 shows that almost half (47.4%) of the senior managers and 30% of the class teachers in the sample reported that they were not obliged to teach IT. Of those respondents who stated that they were obliged to teach IT the majority attributed this to the requirements of the national curriculum. The other responses concerning who or what obliges them to teach IT were the head teacher, school policy, IT being part of the course they taught, job description, and self-obligation.

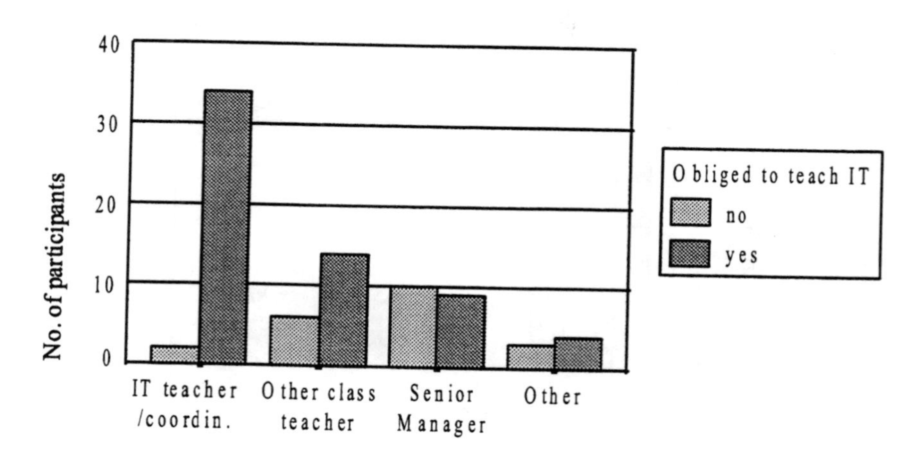

Figure 5.5 – The number of participants in each job category who reported that they were obliged to teach IT

Figure 5.6 shows that the questionnaire respondents were initially trained to teach a wide range of subjects and that only one teacher was initially trained to teach IT. Figure 5.7 shows that the majority (55.6%) of the ICT co-ordinators and IT teachers in the sample were initially trained to teach science. However, there were also those who were initially trained to teach humanities, arts, and primary subjects. Again only one was trained to teach IT initially. This may be due to the majority of the teachers having been a teacher for some time and therefore they would have been trained before initial teacher training courses with IT as the main subject began in 1996. This finding is very important as it indicates that many IT teachers are disadvantaged by not having been trained initially to teach their subject. In many cases, it is likely that they may not have followed a degree course in their current subject either. This implies that IT and ICT teachers/co-ordinators are even more in need of training in the teaching of ICT than their colleagues.

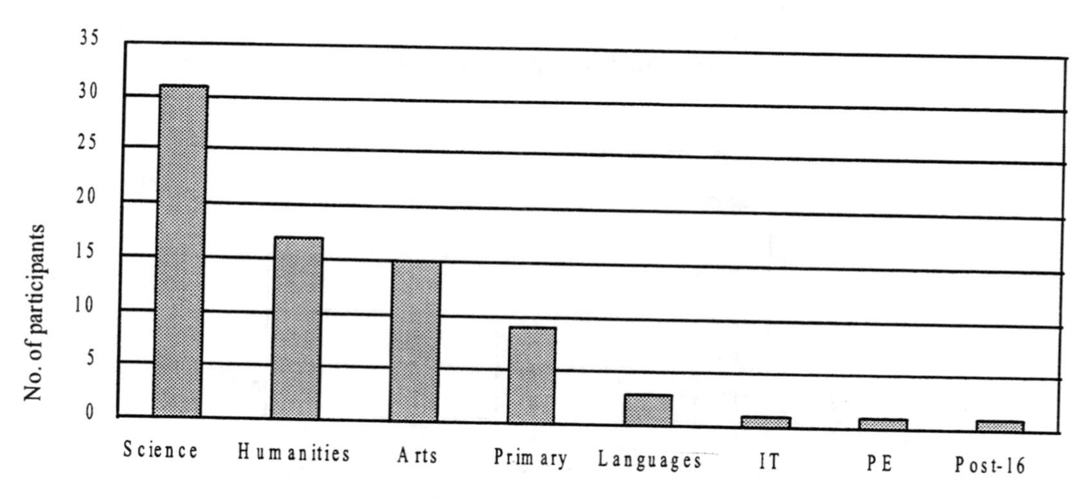

Figure 5.6 – Subjects that the respondents were initially trained to teach

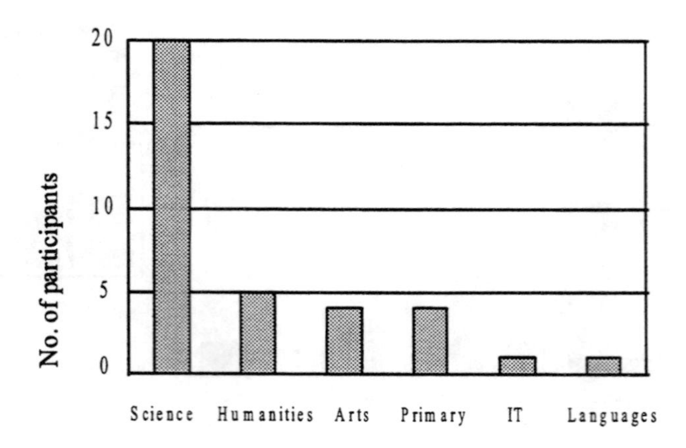

Figure 5.7 - Subjects that the IT teachers and ICT co-ordinators were initially trained to teach

5.2 Personal ICT use

Only three (3.7%) of the teachers from the questionnaire sample did not have access to a computer at home. This compares with results from another recent study by Kim (2000) who found that 53.4% of a sample of 73 teachers had access to a computer at home, thus confirming that our sample was of higher than average users of ICT in the UK and therefore not representative of the teacher population as a whole. This may suggest a relationship between ICT access outside of school and its use in teaching. Furthermore, over three-quarters of the sample (75.6%) reported having access to the Internet outside of school. However, one of the prerequisites for being part of the study was that they had to have an e-mail address, thus indicating that they were experienced ICT users, and consequently we would expect their home computer use to be above the national average for teachers.

Over half the questionnaire sample (54.9%) reported that they owned the computer they used outside of school with another 23.1% stating that it was owned by their partner or family. For 11 (13.4%) of the teachers the computer they used at home was owned by their school. Over half of the respondents (52.5%) shared their computer with one person or was the only user.

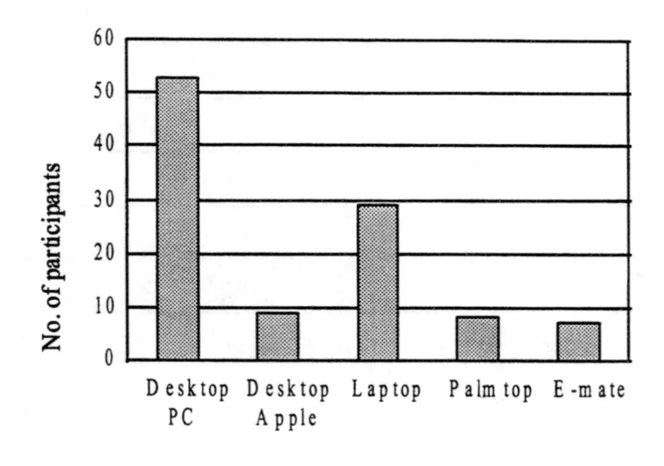

Figure 5.8 – Type of computers used outside of school

The teachers utilised a number of different types of computers for their personal use at home (see Figure 5.8). The majority had a desktop PC or Apple Mac (75.6%), but a large part of the sample owned a laptop computer. A few of the participants had more than one computer for their personal use.

The respondents were asked about their basic ICT skills, which were identified from the Department of Education and Employment's Initial Teacher Training National Curriculum for the use of ICT within subject teaching requirements (1998c). The results are shown in Figure 5.9. These findings show that the majority of the sample was able to perform a wide range of tasks indicating an above average level of ICT skills in relation to other teachers, as reported by OFSTED (Goldstein, 1997) and other previous studies. Figure 5.10 shows that the vast majority of the questionnaire respondents reported using many different forms of ICT at home, including word-processing, spreadsheets, CD-ROM software, and databases. Other uses reported by a minority of teachers included presentation software, digital cameras, music software, video conferencing, and scanning and image manipulation.

The respondents were asked which form of ICT they used most frequently outside of work. Figure 5.11 shows that, for the vast majority of teachers in our sample, the form of ICT used most frequently at home was word-processing. The second and third most frequently used forms of ICT were reported as being desktop publishing and e-mail.

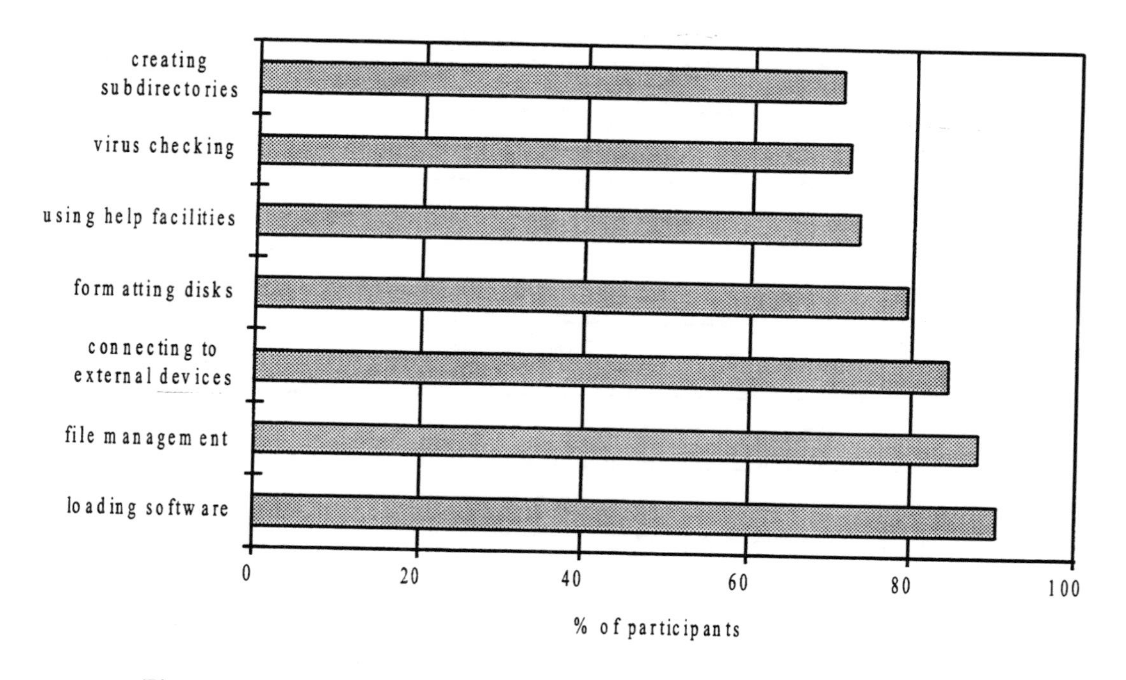

Figure 5.9 - Tasks performed on the teachers' computers outside of school

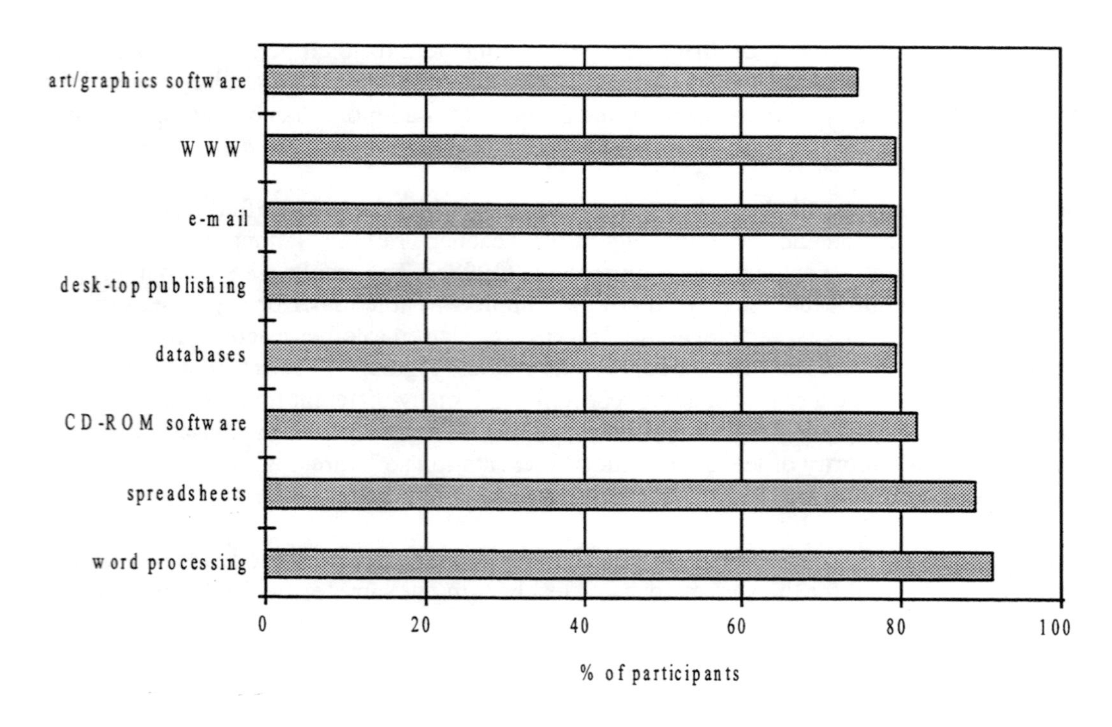

Figure 5.10 – Forms of ICT used outside of school

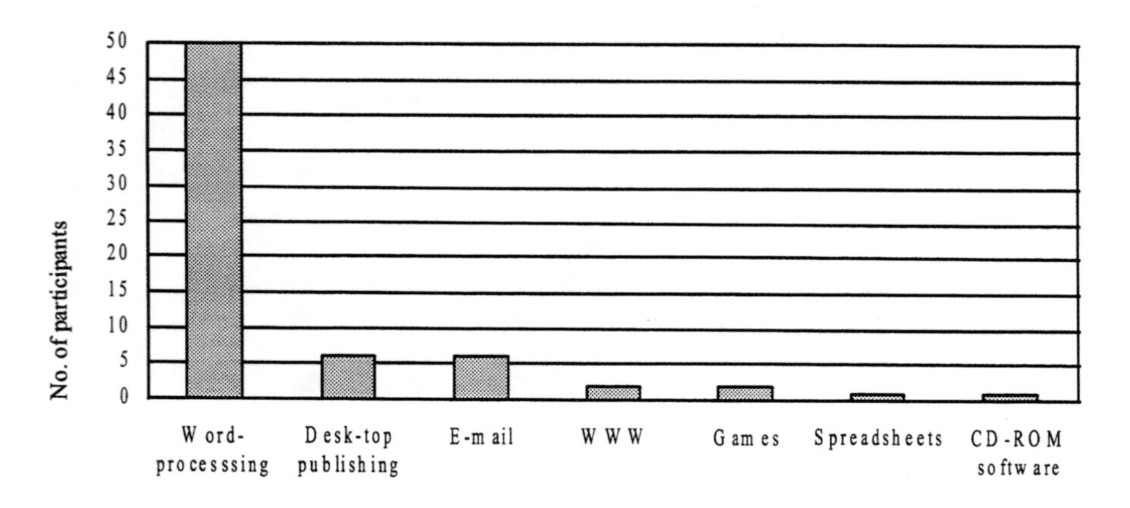

Figure 5.11 - Most frequently used forms of ICT outside of school

The teachers used a wide range of Internet service providers, including AOL, Demon, Freeserve, Compuserve and Edex. The majority of the respondents used Netscape or Internet Explorer software to access the WWW outside of work. Figures 5.12 and 5.13 show that the majority of respondents spent between 0 and 6 hours a week on line for personal use and received and sent between 1 to 20 messages a week. However, the questionnaire responses were obtained in the summer of 1998 and since then there have been significant changes in terms of the Internet services that are available, with the introduction of many free access services. Therefore, it is likely that this has had an impact on the service providers that are used and the amount of time spent on line.

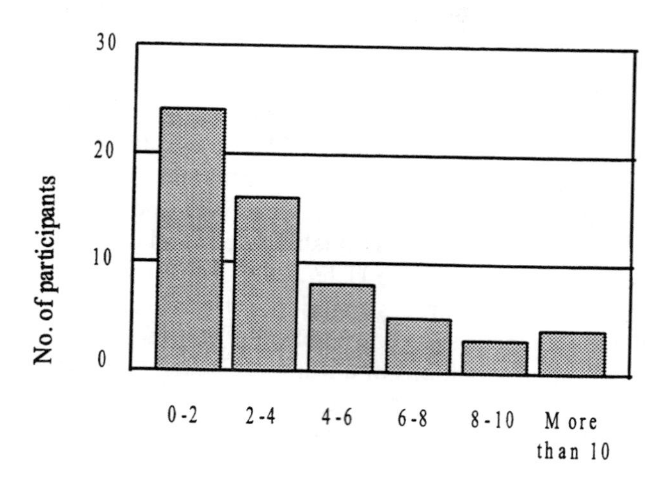

Figure 5.12 – Average number of hours spent on line for personal use each week

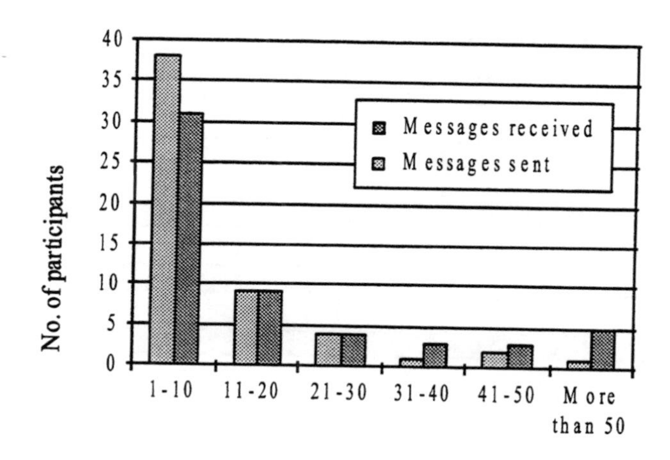

Figure 5.13 – Average number of personal messages received and sent each week

A wide range of web sites was visited frequently by the teachers for their personal use. The most popular types of web sites were search engines, newspapers and those relating to music, sport, and travel. The most popular education web sites were BBC, National Grid for Learning (NGfL), Virtual Teachers' Centre (VTC), DfEE, British Educational and Communications Technology Agency (BECTa), and MirandaNet.

The evidence in this section shows that the majority of the teachers in the sample use a wide range of ICT applications for their personal use. Furthermore, the questionnaire findings suggest that the teachers had substantial expertise in ICT, including using e-mail and the Internet for both personal and professional uses. However, these findings do not necessarily imply that the teachers would use ICT extensively in their teaching. The questionnaire respondents' usage of ICT in their teaching work is discussed in the next section.

5.3 ICT use in teaching

Figure 5.14 shows that the majority of teachers use a wide range of forms of ICT in their teaching. The most popular were word-processing, CD-ROM software, spreadsheets and subject-specific software. These results show that the teachers were including most aspects of the ICT curriculum into their teaching, i.e. communications, handling information, modelling and simulations, and presenting information (Qualifications and Curriculum Authority, 2000). However, although 44% of the sample were IT teachers or ICT co-ordinators, relatively few were using software other than word processing, desk-top publishing and CD-ROM software more than one hour per month, as is shown in Table 5.1. This lack of variation in the forms of ICT used is supported by the observations of a MirandaNet fellow: "Most of my staff are using the computers only for word processing, spelling games in literacy hour and other games at play times" (head teacher of a primary school). However, the majority of teachers wanted to use more educational software in their teaching, indicating that they were motivated to use ICT more frequently but were unable to do so due to insufficient time, inadequate resources, and so on.

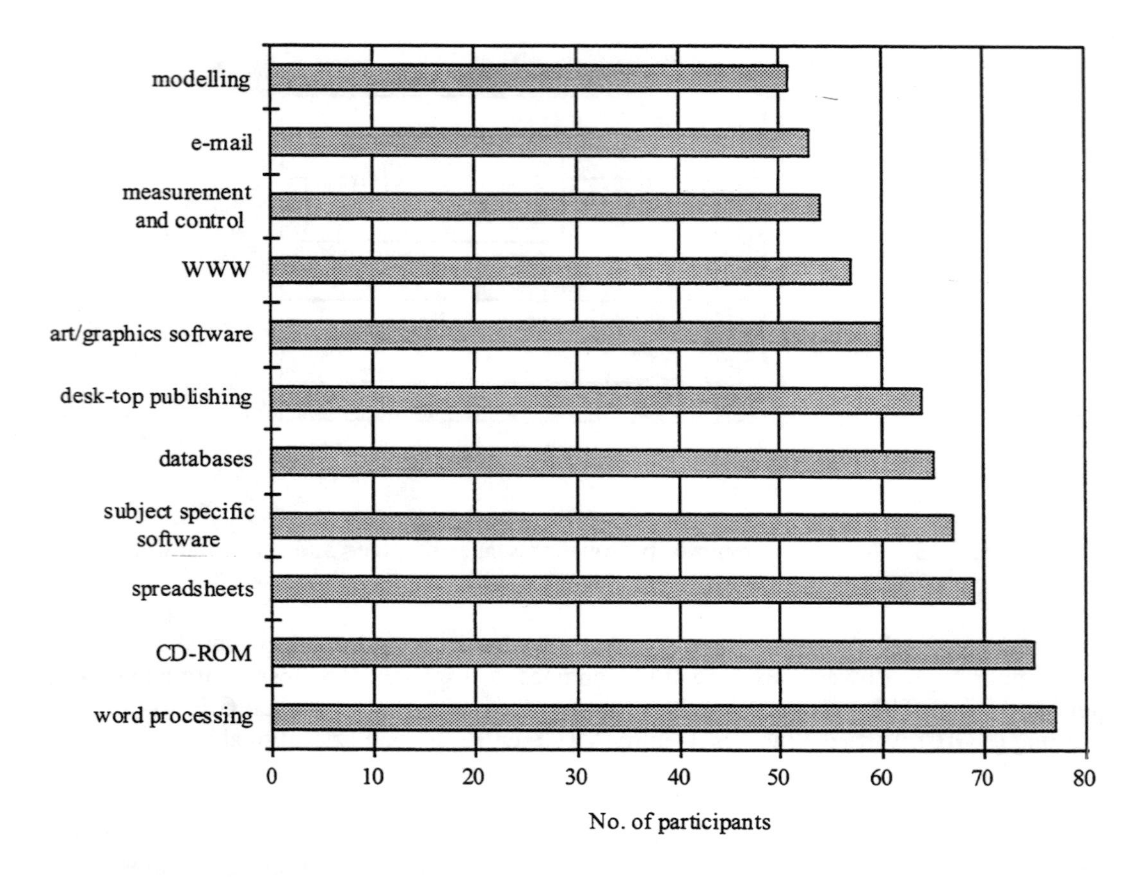

Figure 5.14 – Number of questionnaire participants who use various forms of ICT in their teaching

Table 5.1 – Average (median) frequency of using different forms of ICT in teaching

Several hours each week	An hour each week	An hour each month
Word-processing	Desk-top publishing	Spreadsheets
	CD-ROM software	Databases
		Art/graphics software
		Modelling
		Measurement and control
		Subject specific software
		E-mail
		WWW

5.4 Attitudes to using ICT in teaching

Drawing on the discussion of theoretical models developed and used by previous researchers (see section 3.1) we have adopted two components from the model of Davis, Bagozzi and Warshaw (1989), namely *perceived ease of use* and *perceived usefulness*. From the analysis of the MirandaNet documents and previous research we identified several factors relating to each component. These factors were then investigated further through specific items in the questionnaire. The responses to these questionnaire items and other evidence from the MirandaNet data are discussed below.

In this section some of the data are presented in horizontal bar charts, whereby each bar is divided into sections to indicate the percentage of participants who gave each particular response. Therefore, for example, in Figure 5.15 the top bar shows the responses the teachers gave to the item "hardware/software problems often disrupt lessons". The graph shows that 5.3% strongly disagreed with this statement, 30.7% disagreed, 29.3% were neutral, 28.0% agreed and 6.7% strongly agreed.

5.4.1 Perceived ease of use

For the purpose of our analyses we have defined *ease of use* as teachers' perceptions of factors which hinder/support their use of ICT. (We are focusing on *ease of use* in terms of ICT use in teaching only, not personal or other kinds of use). Previous research suggests that there are many factors that act as barriers to ICT use, i.e. they decrease the ease of use of ICT in teaching, thus preventing teachers from using ICT regularly. For example, Sinko and Lehtinen (1999) found that some teachers consider the difficulties experienced in using hardware/software to be a reason for not using ICT in their teaching. Therefore, the questionnaire respondents were asked to rate the extent to which they agreed with six statements concerning factors which make using ICT in their teaching more difficult. The responses to these items, shown in Figure 5.15, indicate that most respondents (between 62.7 and 82.4%) disagree that these factors are significant barriers to using ICT in their teaching, with the exception of difficulties with hardware/software disrupting lessons and preparation for lessons being time consuming.

According to previous research, discussed in section 3, teachers often report that in order to use ICT on a regular basis they need substantial technical and human support. We therefore expected that their perceived need for more support might have a significant effect on ease of use and so we asked the teachers to rate the extent to which they felt they needed various forms of support. Figure 5.16 shows the range of responses concerning the perceived need for more technical and staff support, more resources and more time. The majority felt that they had insufficient technical support, time and ICT resources, with 50% being dissatisfied with the level of ICT resources to which they have access. 30% of the respondents agreed that using ICT could be counterproductive if there were insufficient resources, as is shown in Figure 5.17.

In contradiction to the Davis, Bagozzi and Warshaw model, our research shows that ease of use relating to support is not a very influential factor, as the majority of the respondents use ICT in their teaching on a regular basis even though they do not feel that they have sufficient resources, time, or technical support. This suggests that, on balance, the respondents found they were able to use ICT in their teaching despite their inadequate support and resources.

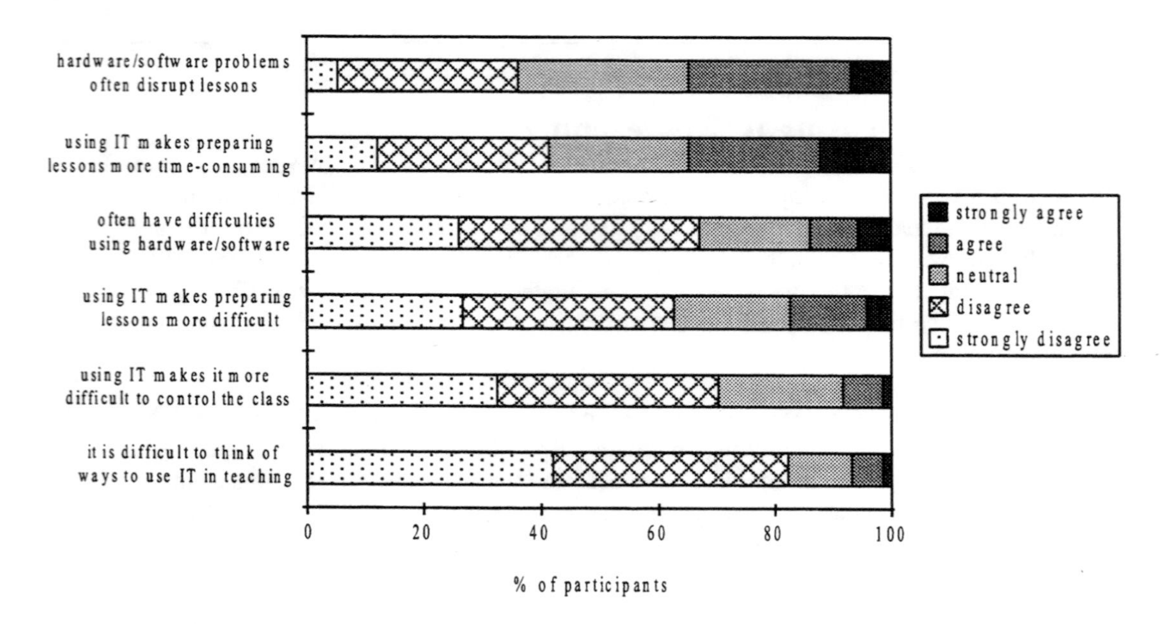

Figure 5.15 – Responses to the items relating to ease of use of ICT in teaching

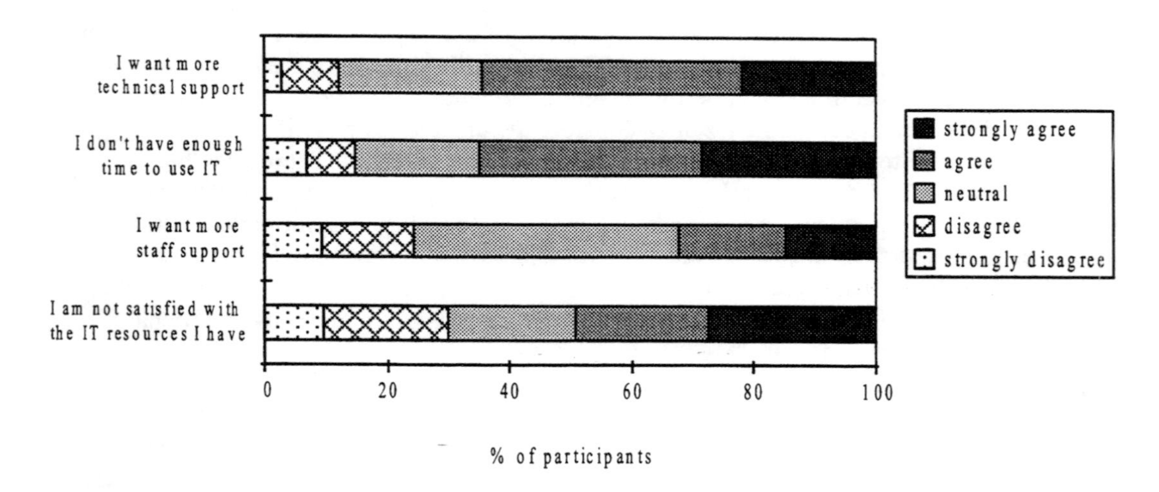

Figure 5.16 – Responses to the items relating to the need for more support

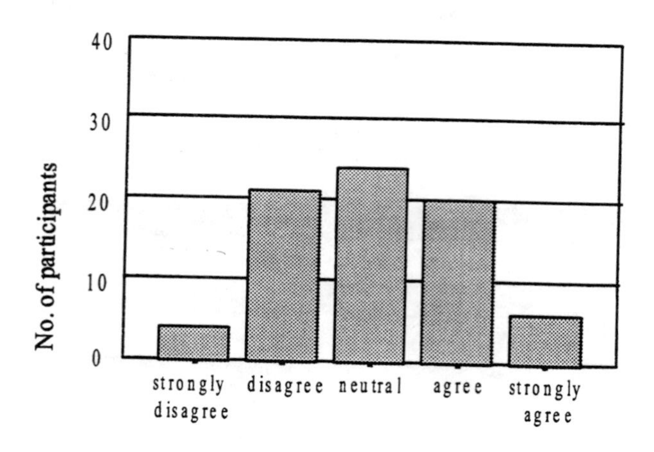

Figure 5.17 – Responses to the item "Using IT in my teaching can be counter-productive due to insufficient technical resources"

5.4.2 Perceived usefulness

We have examined three aspects relating to the perceived usefulness of using ICT in teaching, namely the impact on teaching, on pupils and on the teachers themselves.

Impact on teaching

To assess the usefulness for teaching we asked the teachers questions concerning whether ICT use affected the quality of their lessons, such as the diversity or content, and whether it made teaching more enjoyable, interesting and so on. The responses to these questions are shown in Figure 5.18. The results show that the great majority agreed that using ICT makes their lessons more enjoyable, interesting, diverse, and fun. According to the work of Weiner (1990) and Ames (1992), discussed in Cox (1997), these are all indications of positive motivation, showing that the teachers in our sample were motivated to use ICT in their teaching.

Impact on pupils

Previous research (e.g. Ames, 1992) suggests that teachers are often persuaded to adopt innovations if they believe that these innovations will have a positive effect on the pupils. Consequently, we included items in the questionnaire to assess the extent to which the teachers felt that using ICT in their teaching benefited the pupils. Over 85% of the respondents agreed that ICT makes their lessons more fun for the pupils, aids pupils' learning, and increases pupils' motivation (see Figure 5.19). This demonstrates that they believed that ICT was greatly beneficial for their pupils, indicating that this might be a motivational factor.

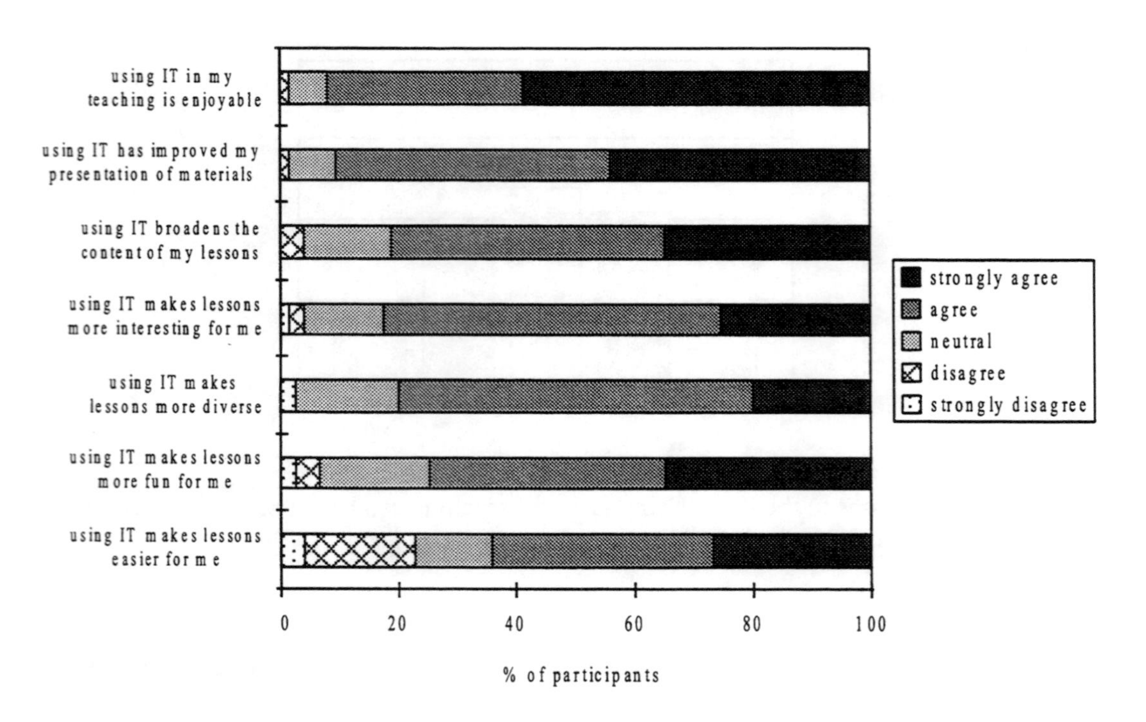

Figure 5.18 – Responses to the items relating to the impact of using ICT on teaching

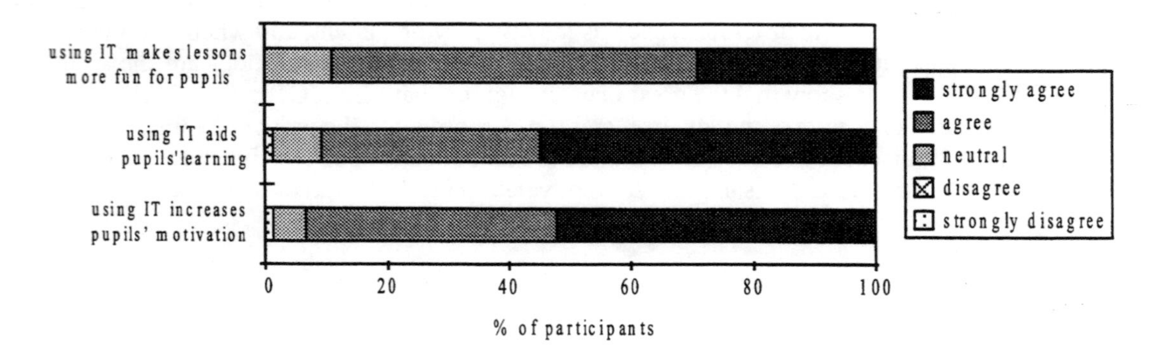

Figure 5.19 – Responses to the items relating to the impact of using ICT on pupils

Impact on self

In addition to the questionnaire items concerning the usefulness of using ICT for teaching and for the pupils, we were also interested in the impact on teachers, both professionally and personally. Figure 5.20 shows the responses to the six factors that were identified by the MirandaNet documents as being important to the teachers regarding the benefits of using ICT in their teaching for their personal and professional use. The most important of these were found to be having a greater awareness of the uses of ICT, having more confidence in using ICT and greater access for personal ICT use. Almost half the participants agreed that using ICT in their teaching enhanced their career prospects, whilst some respondents also agreed that it gave them more prestige and more power within their school. However, as many of the respondents already held senior positions in their school we would not expect them to feel that using ICT gave them greater career prospects, more power or more prestige. Only a small minority (less than 20%) disagreed with any of the factors relating to perceived usefulness for the teachers' personal or professional development.

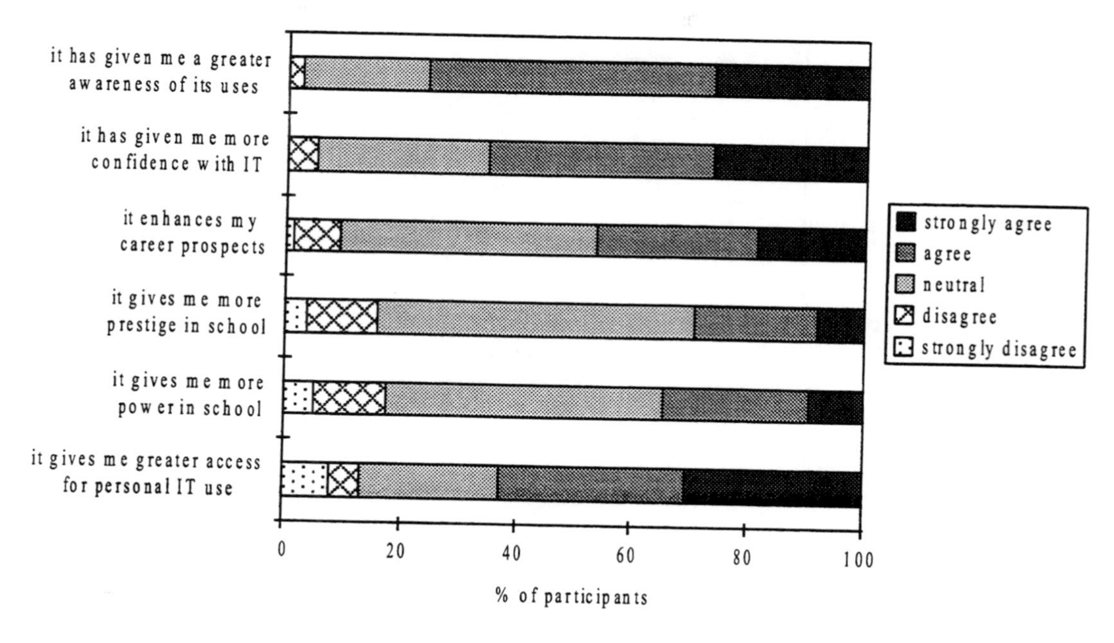

Figure 5.20 – Responses to the items relating to the impact of using ICT on the teacher and his/her professional development

Due to the many changes in education introduced by the UK government in recent years there have been marked increases in the amount of administration work that teachers are required to undertake. Therefore, the belief of the majority of the respondents that ICT has made their administration more efficient (see Figure 5.21) indicates that this may be a strong motivational factor for using ICT. Use of ICT for administration tasks may also have the resultant effect of increasing its use in other ways, i.e. in the teachers' teaching or personal use. The respondents did, however, mostly agree that using ICT in teaching was expensive (see Figure 5.22), which clearly is affected by the amount of resources that are available to them. The need for using ICT in teaching to be more affordable is emphasised by a MirandaNet fellow. "(The) big challenge is to find a display system for a class that is affordable, without which ICT cannot really be used as a whole-class teaching aid (which has so many possibilities). This is urgent" (Director of a school ICT training centre).

The evidence discussed above shows that there was a range of factors that contributed to the teachers' perceived usefulness of ICT. The most important of these were benefits for pupils and for their teaching. Over 90% of the respondents agree that using ICT increases pupils' motivation, aids pupils' learning, makes the lessons more fun and their teaching more enjoyable. Other aspects of usefulness agreed by many of the respondents, such as making lessons more diverse, making the users aware of its potential and improving the users' confidence, all provide strong indications of the importance of perceived usefulness in motivating the teachers to use ICT. These findings demonstrate that a large majority of teachers use ICT in their teaching not just because they are obliged to, due to school policy, their professional role, etc., but because they find it useful and beneficial for both them and their pupils.

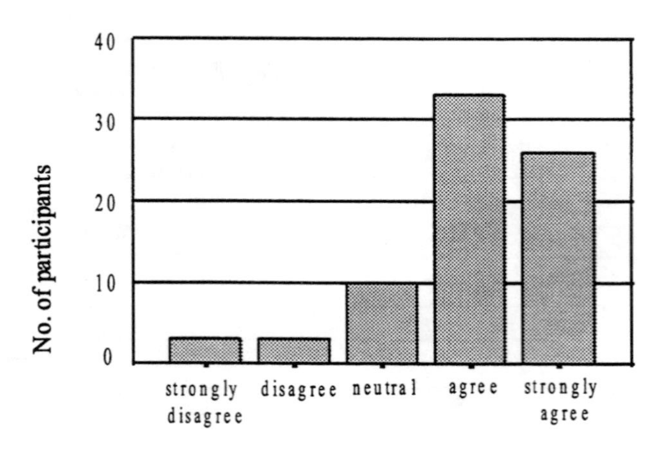

Figure 5.21 – Responses to the item "Using IT in my teaching makes my administration more efficient"

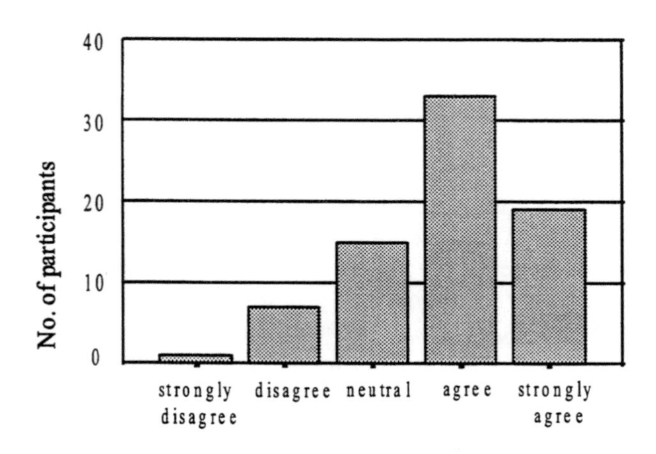

Figure 5.22 – Responses to the item "Using IT in my teaching is often highly expensive"

5.5 Advantages and disadvantages of using ICT in teaching

In addition to asking the teachers to rate the extent to which they agreed with the particular statements about using ICT in their teaching (see section 5.4), we also asked them to state what they considered to be the main advantages and disadvantages. Their responses are discussed in the following two sections.

5.5.1 Advantages of using ICT in teaching

The individual responses that were given concerning the advantages of using ICT in teaching fell into two main categories: those relating to the pupils and those benefits for the teachers themselves.

a. Advantages for the pupils

The majority of the teachers' responses concerning the advantages of using ICT referred to benefits for the pupils, with increased motivation being the most common. For example, one teacher noted that "IT provides excellent motivational factors for children who sometimes lack confidence, ability or presentation skills". This suggests that the benefits for pupils may be a major motivating factor for the teachers leading to sustained use of ICT. Some teachers also suggested that using ICT increases pupils' interest and enhances their concentration and that they find it enjoyable and fun. One teacher noted that "using ICT brings lots of knowledge and info. alive". Another argued that "providing that there is sufficient hardware, students concentrate to their full capacity because there is little peer group distraction".

Advantages due to the impact of ICT on pupils' ability to learn were also given, as pupils have more control of their learning and using ICT supports the needs of the individual learner. For example, respondents stated that using ICT "enables the student to find the style of learning that suits them" and "empowers the whole ability range". The importance of ICT in today's society was also inferred by some teachers who felt that using ICT in their teaching provides pupils with the necessary ICT skills and prepares them for their future in a technology based society. For example, one participant declared that using ICT "gives students opportunities to use valuable skills they will need in their future careers". Finally, many teachers stated that using ICT improves the presentation of pupils' work enabling "all pupils to achieve a satisfying, professional looking result".

b. Advantages for the teachers

The remaining responses referred to the advantages of using ICT in their teaching for the teachers themselves. Many of the teachers' responses related to using ICT to improve their teaching by increasing the teaching strategies available and diversifying activities. This appeared to increase the teachers' enjoyment of their lessons, as one teacher notes "a greater variety of approaches to the same subject area makes it more interesting for me". It was also suggested that using ICT can often make it easier to focus on the learning task rather than on the process. For example, according to one respondent, ICT is a "tool that can increase the quality of learning by keeping the focus on the learning objective and not the process of researching/presenting/collating information". In addition, some teachers also suggested that it makes some tasks easier or faster, improves the presentation of their materials, and allows them to do things that they wouldn't be able to do otherwise, such as "enhance the recording of data that's otherwise difficult to accurately record". Finally, the advancement of the Internet has provided teachers with "more diverse and better materials" to use in their teaching.

5.5.2 Disadvantages of using ICT in teaching

The responses that were given concerning the disadvantages of using ICT in teaching fell into six main categories. The greatest disadvantage was reported to be inadequate resources and support.

a. Inadequate resources and support

A number of difficulties due to inadequate resources and support were stated. Many of the teachers reported that there was not enough access to computers for ICT to be used as often as they would like and that there were difficulties associated with needing to reserve access to ICT resources beforehand as careful planning was needed to accommodate every teacher's needs. Other teachers also stated that when they did have access to computers there were not enough for all the class. For example, one teacher said that she "is always short of hardware for students (and) therefore course-work etc. can be slow to accomplish". Some of the teachers also complained about out of date resources and about "how quickly hardware gets obsolete". This was also considered to be problematic due to the higher quality of some of the pupils' ICT equipment at home. Finally, some teachers felt that they did not have enough technical support to use ICT effectively in their teaching.

b. Technical problems

Many teachers stated that technical problems were a disadvantage of using them in their teaching, which in many cases was related to a lack of adequate resources discussed above. One teacher felt that "poorly specified and maintained machines mean that they are unreliable and likely to cause disruption to even the best planned lessons". It was also argued that technical problems can result in the "demotivation of students" and the removal of "time/resources from other important curriculum areas".

c. Time

Some of the teachers stated that using ICT in their teaching was time-consuming in terms of the preparation necessary and also during the lessons. In terms of preparation, one teacher reported feeling "somewhat frustrated given (his) full teaching load (as he) cannot explore/prepare more materials for children's use on the computer as (it is) time-consuming". Another teacher reported that using ICT in his teaching "creates a great deal of work preparing accurate materials which can be used by a range of abilities". In relation to the extra time needed during lessons one teacher argued that "it is sometimes difficult finding time for all the children to experience a particular piece of IT work".

d. Cost of resources

The cost of ICT was claimed by many of the teachers to be a major disadvantage of using ICT in their teaching. It was also stated that this resulted in low availability of resources for students, which is discussed above.

e. The extra supervision necessary

Some of the responses concerning the disadvantages of using ICT in teaching related to the need for extra supervision. Some teachers reported that there were difficulties involved in teaching large groups all at the same time, and that one to one supervision was often necessary. Other teachers suggested that when using ICT lessons can be difficult to co-ordinate and manage, partly because students can often be distracted from lesson activity. One teacher also claimed that "it is difficult to be sure of pupils' personal contributions".

f. Inadequate training

A few of the teachers felt that they had not had adequate training for using ICT, particularly relating to their ability to solve technical problems, knowledge of "how it works" and experience of software. Other teachers argued that there was a lack of investment in staff training, that training can be time-consuming, and that it is difficult to overcome teachers' fears in their abilities.

Two other disadvantages of using ICT in teaching noted by individual teachers were that there is too much focus on word-processing rather than using ICT in a wider range of tasks, and that girls can be "turned off" learning by its use. Finally, it is worth stating that three of the questionnaire respondents reported that there were no disadvantages of using ICT in their teaching at all.

5.6 Using the Internet in teaching

In view of the rolling out of the National Grid for Learning, the utilisation of the Internet required in teaching and the anticipated emphasis on the Internet for in-service training, we collected evidence of the respondents' current uses of the Internet in their teaching. Figure 5.23 shows that the respondents are using the Internet in a variety of locations, the most common place being at home, followed by in the classroom. The vast majority of teachers in our study had access to the Internet, however, as one MirandaNet fellow points out, in the teaching population as a whole, many teachers do not have access. "(There is a) big concern about schools and individuals that have not got access yet... I am on several mailing lists, but it is clear that the vast majority of teachers do not have easy access yet" (Director of a school ICT training centre).

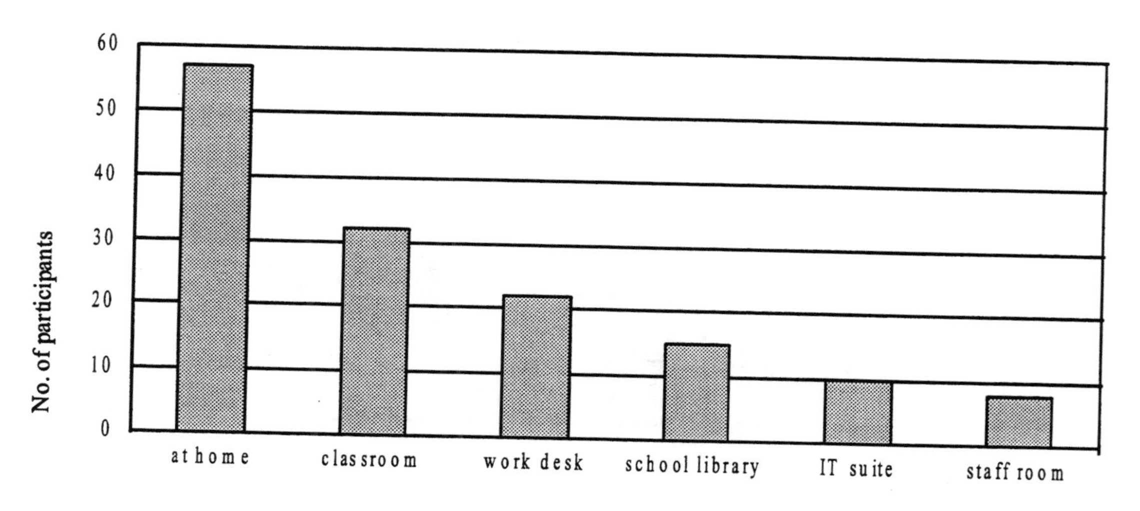

Figure 5.23 – Where the teachers obtain access to the Internet

The questionnaire respondents were asked to estimate the percentage of staff and pupils at their institution who had e-mail addresses at home and at school. The findings are shown in Figures 5.24 and 5.25. For the majority of the respondents less than 25% of the staff in their institution had e-mail addresses at school or at home, with only 18 institutions having more than 75% of staff with e-mail addresses at school. A similar pattern was found for the pupils, with the majority of respondents reporting that less than 25% of pupils in their institutions had e-mail addresses at school or at home. However, as discussed earlier, these responses were obtained in the summer of 1998, i.e. before the widespread introduction of the National Grid for Learning in schools. In addition, a previous report by the British Educational Suppliers Association (1998) showed that there was a very rapid increase in the number of schools gaining access to the Internet between 1995 and 1998 and it is likely that this trend will continue. Therefore, it is probable that the percentage of staff and pupils with regular access to the Internet will now be greater than demonstrated by our present results.

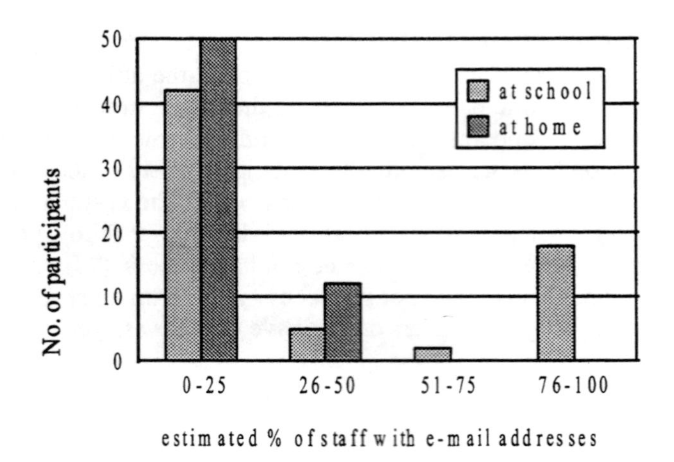

Figure 5.24 – Estimated % of the other staff in the respondents' institutions who have e-mail addresses at home and at school

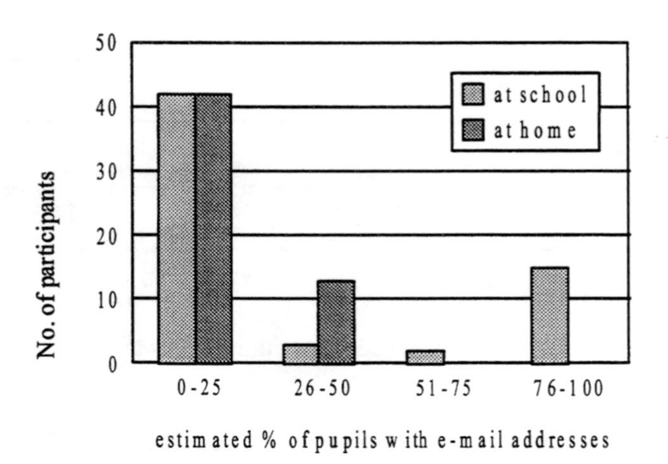

Figure 5.25 – Estimated % of the pupils in the respondents' institutions who have e-mail addresses at home and at school

Through our examination of the MirandaNet materials we identified the 12 most popular web sites for professional use. The questionnaire respondents were asked whether they valued these web sites and also what other web sites they found useful. Figure 5.26 shows that out of these 12, the BBC web site was valued by the greatest number of participants. In addition to those web sites shown in this figure, the DfEE's web site was also deemed to be useful by some respondents. Furthermore, a few of the respondents belonged to on-line discussion groups or used listservs. These included MirandaNet, BBC, Teacher to Teacher, Compuserve education, and Virtual Teachers' Centre section for senior managers.

Only 22% reported that they had used video conferencing. This form of ICT had been used for various purposes including the delivery of A levels by distance learning; the simultaneous performance of a play with a school in Japan; conference sessions with the Science Museum; communication with other schools in England and other countries; and having pupils learn sociology though a college elsewhere.

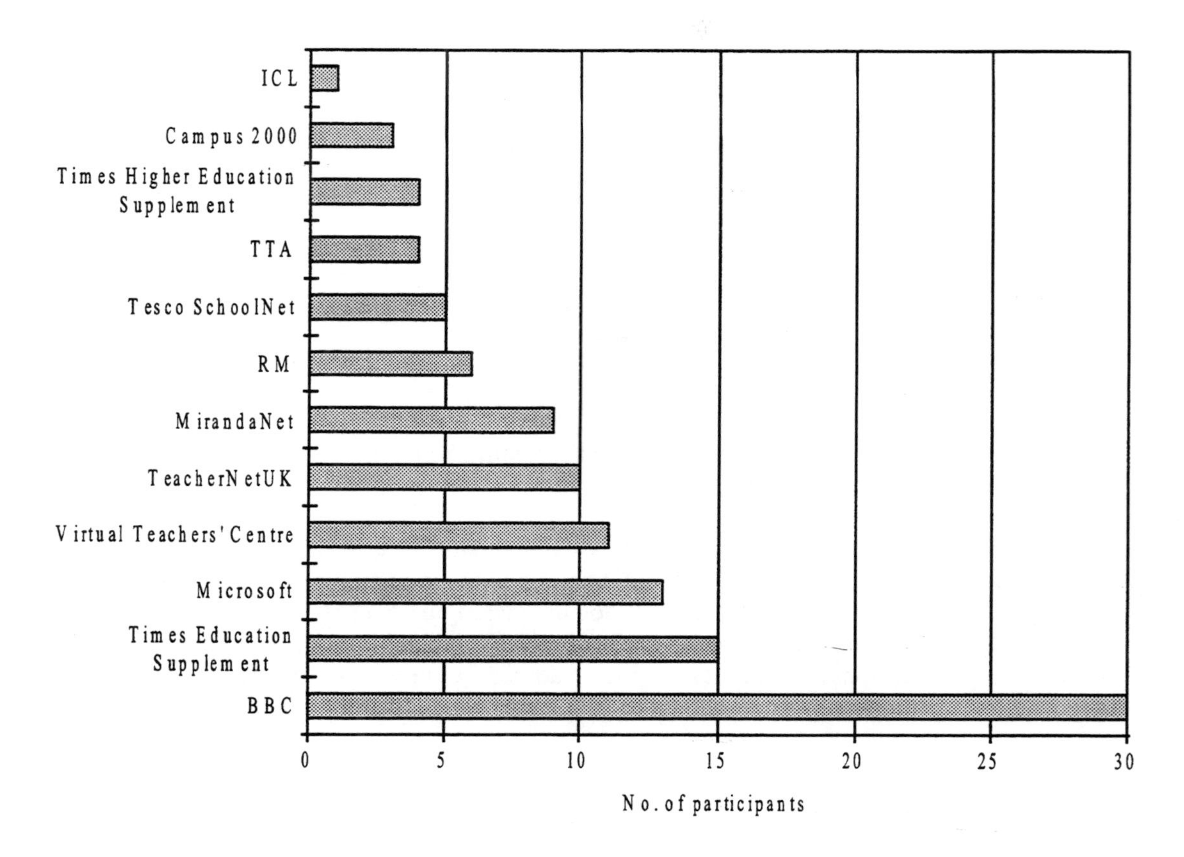

Figure 5.26 – Web sites that were highly valued for professional use (in 1998/1999)

Half the participants said that, if provided with sufficient training, they would be willing to spend about 15 hours a month tutoring colleagues from other institutions through on-line communication. 19.5% were uncertain. Some of the teachers did state that they would only be willing to do this if they were to receive some financial reward for providing such tuition. Nevertheless, this finding indicates that many teachers view this form of professional development as being highly useful and worthwhile as they are willing to give up a substantial proportion of their time to help other teachers improve their use of ICT in their teaching. Of course, many of the MirandaNet members in the sample already do this as part of their membership.

Although some of the respondents had indicated that they did not need more technical or staff support for using ICT in their teaching (see Figure 5.16), Figure 5.27 shows that a large majority were interested in being a member of an on-line support network. This indicates that they value being part of an ICT community and are interested in giving/receiving support of this kind. The value of such communities is demonstrated by a member of the MirandaNet on-line support network, who argues that "it seems foolish to attempt to work on ICT development in isolation when, with a little communication, ideas can be shared, discussed and refined" (teacher of design and technology and co-ordinator of staff ICT training at a comprehensive school). Further advantages of MirandaNet are discussed in section 5.9.

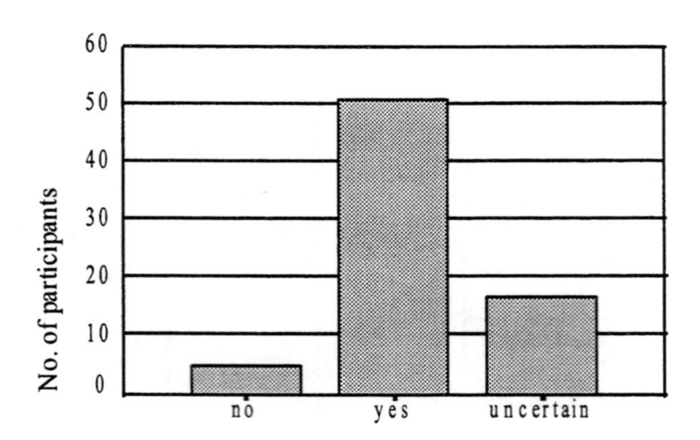

Figure 5.27 – The number of participants who would like to be a member of an on-line support network for teachers

In order to explore how teachers can benefit by using the Internet, the respondents were asked to rate, on a scale of 1 (low value) to 5 (high value), the value of a range of Internet facilities, which were identified from the MirandaNet documents. Figure 5.28 shows that those that were considered to be the most important related to the teachers' knowledge and expertise, e.g. accessing professional resources and getting advice from experts. Features that enabled teachers to publish their own materials or to find employment were considered to be the least valuable.

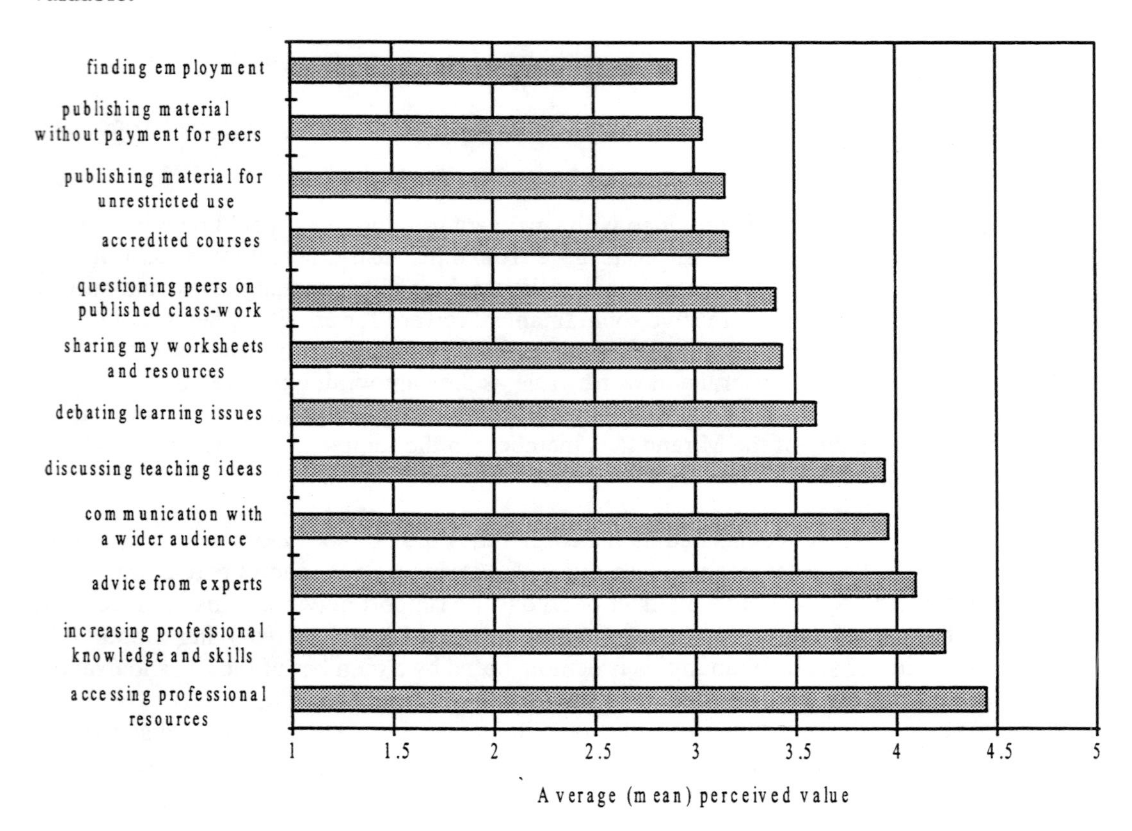

Figure 5.28 – Average (mean) perceived value of different aspects of using the Internet

5.7 National Grid for Learning (NGfL)

Figure 5.29 shows the current position regarding the integration of the NGfL into the questionnaire participants' schools. Although the majority maintained that they would be making substantial use of the NGfL in the future, only 20% stated that they were currently integrating it into their teaching. However, at the time of conducting this research schools were still at the early stages of making use of the NGfL so it is expected that few teachers would have reached the stage at which they have adopted it in their teaching. In fact, 48 (58.5%) of the teachers in the questionnaire sample reported that their institution is developing or has already developed an Intranet for staff and pupils to use. Five (6.1%) of the respondents were uncertain.

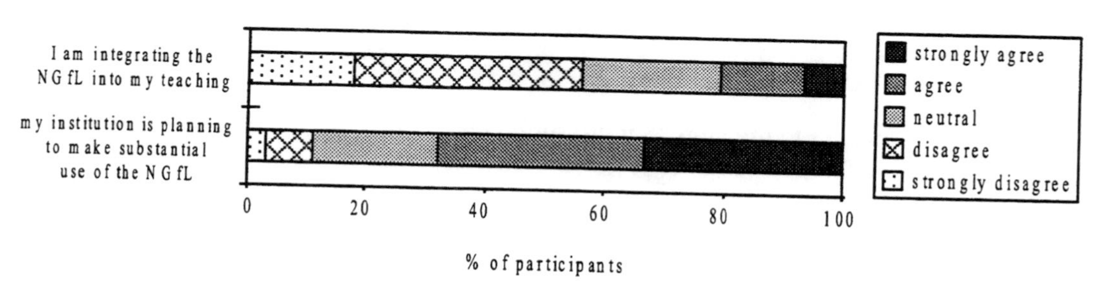

Figure 5.29 – Responses to the items relating to the plans of the teachers and their institutions to use the NGfL

In view of the government's proposal that all teachers and pupils should have e-mail addresses, the teachers who participated in this study were asked the extent to which they thought having e-mail addresses would help teachers and pupils. Figure 5.30 shows that nearly 90% agreed that teachers having an e-mail address would help the teaching profession and 60% believed that pupils having e-mail addresses would help them to learn about ICT.

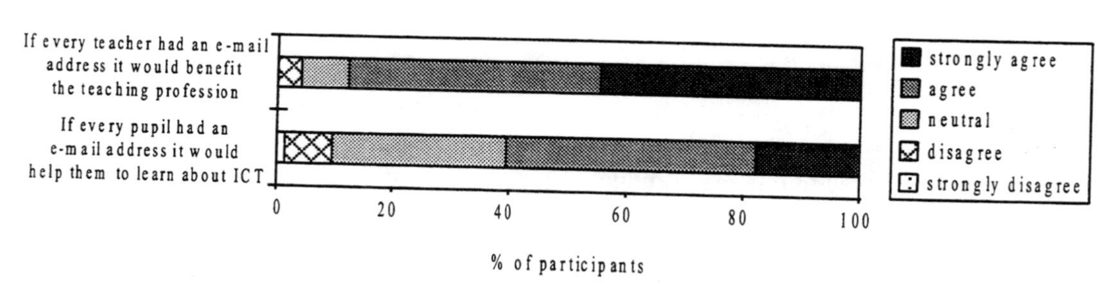

Figure 5.30 – Responses to the items relating to the impact of e-mail addresses on teachers and pupils

Despite this strong support for the NGfL and access to e-mail, a significant minority felt that their institution did not have enough resources to take advantage of the NGfL (Figure 5.31). Furthermore, more than 50% did not think that they were well informed about the NGfL (see Figure 5.32). This is particularly worrying, as the introduction of the NGfL was imminent when this survey was conducted. In addition, if many teachers, like our questionnaire respondents, who have an interest and are experienced in ICT, do not feel well informed about the NGfL, then how prepared are those teachers who do not yet use ICT?

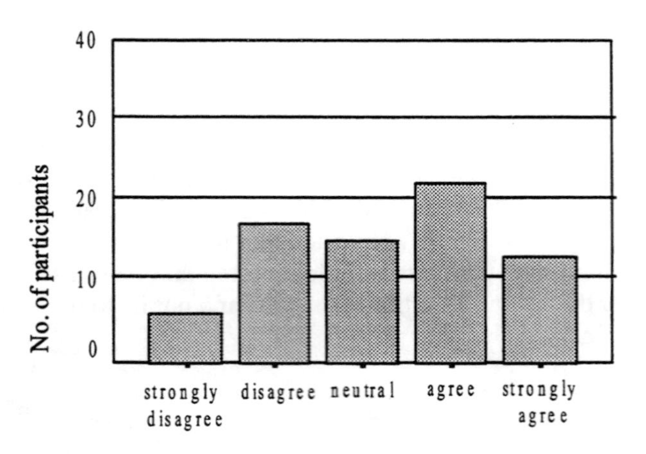

Figure 5.31 – Responses to the item "My institution has enough resources to take advantage of NGfL opportunities"

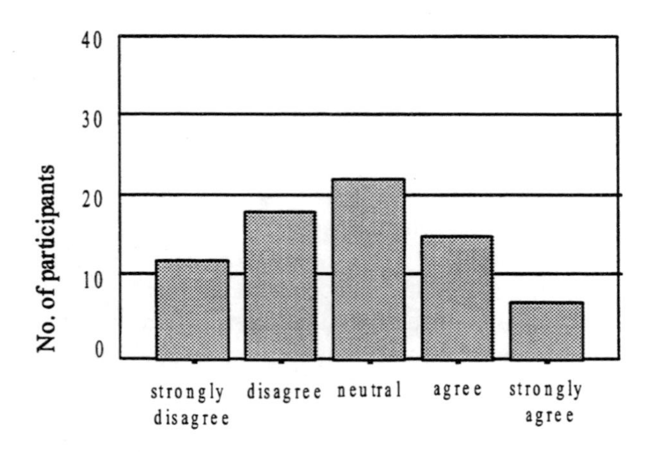

Figure 5.32 – Responses to the item "I am well informed about the NGfL"

The teachers were asked to rate the usefulness of various sources of information on the NGfL, on a scale of 1 (of no use) to 5 (very useful). Figure 5.33 shows the average responses that were given for each source. With the exception of the education and educational computing press and on-line investigations, none were considered to be particularly useful. Sources of information on the NGfL that were deemed to have been useful by a small minority of teachers were MirandaNet, the computer press, the DfEE web site, a co-ordinator for the NGfL project, colleagues from other boroughs already working on the NGfL, the Local Training Enterprise Council, a Research Machines conference video, and students and their enquiries. However, as the NGfL is not yet up and running in all schools the teachers could obviously not know for certain how useful the sources of information would actually be in the future.

The teachers were also asked when pupils should be given addresses in relation to teachers. Figure 5.34 shows that more than 50% agreed that teachers and pupils should be given them simultaneously. The most common reason given for this view was that teachers and pupils learning and working together would result in the Internet becoming an integral part of teaching and learning in schools. It was noted that some pupils may already have the skills and confidence to use e-mail and that this may help and encourage teachers to learn. For example, one teacher, whose school had already used this method, argued that "the notion that teachers must become expert before imparting skills to students has long gone". Another common reason for giving teachers and pupils e-mail at the same time was equal opportunities for both to take advantage of the benefits, as this provides "empowerment for all". Other teachers suggested that providing teachers and pupils with e-mail together would enable and encourage e-mail communication between them.

However, as is shown in Figure 5.34, a large minority felt that teachers should get their e-mail addresses first, as teachers need to develop the necessary skills and confidence. These respondents suggested that this was vital in order for the teachers to be able to help pupils, learn how to use it effectively in their teaching and supervise pupils' activities. A few participants also suggested that if pupils were given e-mail at the same time then this might threaten and undermine the teachers. For example, it was argued that "teachers are scared enough already of kids knowing more than they do" and that teachers "would feel threatened by the pupils' knowledge and this would alienate teachers from using IT". A very small number of teachers thought that pupils should be given e-mail before staff, as this would motivate teachers to learn, or that pupils shouldn't be given e-mail addresses at all as this is costly and their activities may be difficult to supervise.

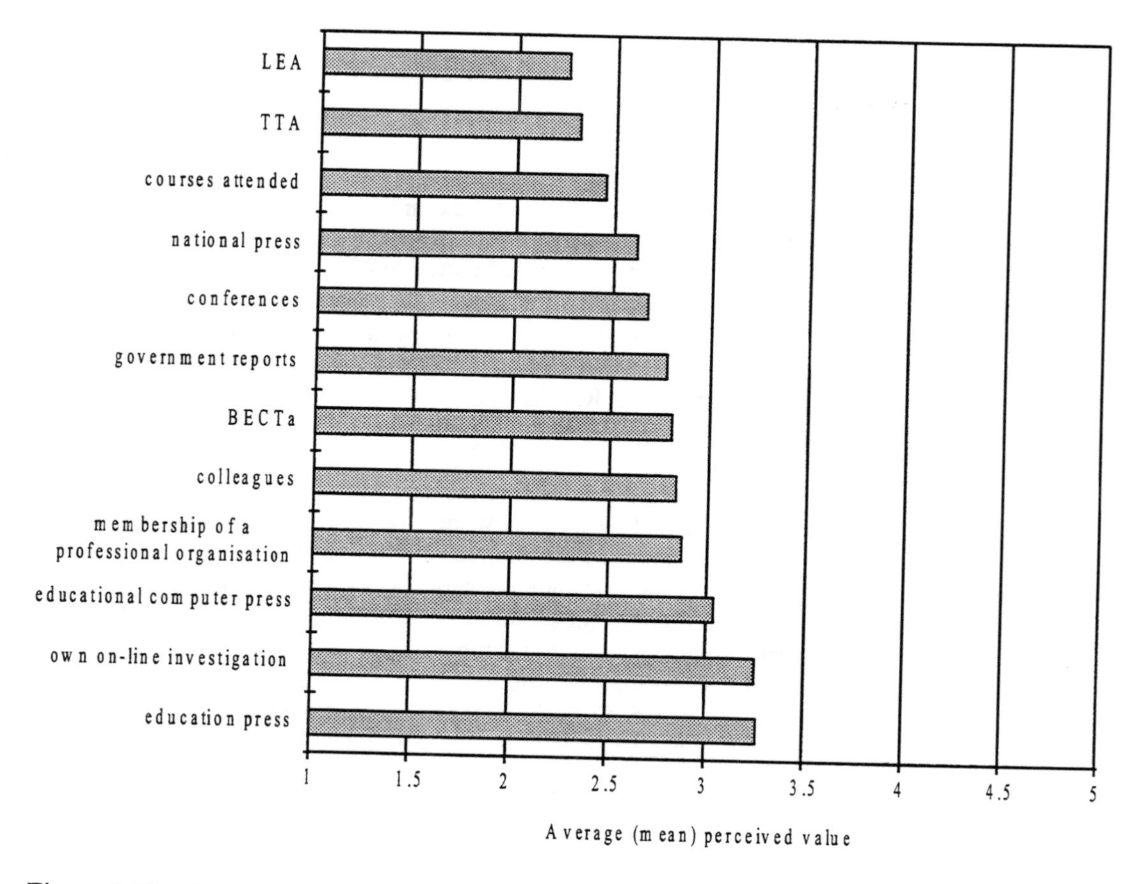

Figure 5.33 – Average (mean) perceived usefulness of different sources of information on the NGfL

We were not able, within the scope of the project, to investigate the teachers' opinions about the potential impact of everyone (i.e. both teachers and pupils) having e-mail addresses on workloads and teacher-pupils communications, although clearly this could have both positive and negative effects on teachers' time and curriculum management.

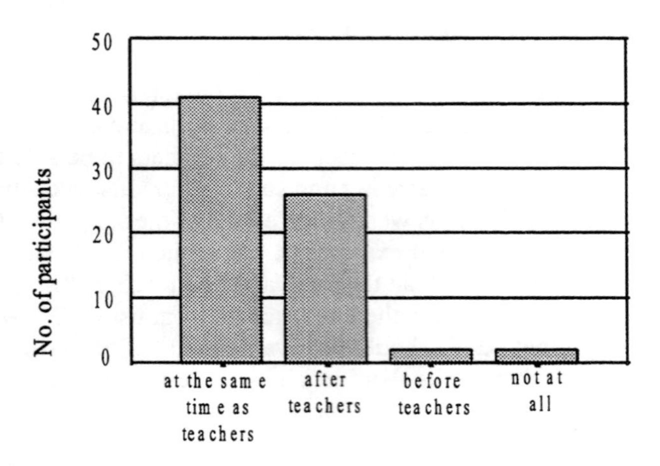

Figure 5.34 – When pupils should be given free e-mail addresses in relation to teachers

5.8 Professional development

Previous research, for example Underwood (1997) and Cox and Rhodes (1990), has shown that the effect of in-service training about the uses of ICT in teaching on subsequent practice depends upon the type, length and location of the course attended. The most effective has been shown to be long certificated courses that address pedagogical practices as well as teaching the participants ICT skills. We therefore included a section in the questionnaire about training and other support received to determine if this had influenced the uptake of ICT in the teaching of our sample of regular ICT users and to explore their views on the benefits of training.

Figure 5.35 shows the number of courses attended by the respondents in the past and Figure 5.36 shows the types of these courses and where they were located. Most had attended at least 3 courses but 11 respondents had not attended any courses at all. Figure 5.36 shows that the courses that were attended by most of the respondents were short special courses at an LEA centre and initial awareness and short courses in school. As was explained earlier in section 5.1, of the 35 ICT co-ordinators and teachers in the sample only one had been trained initially to teach IT, indicating that their only formal training in their subject was through in-service education. This is in contrast to science or English secondary school teachers for example, who usually get a first degree in science or English before training to be a teacher.

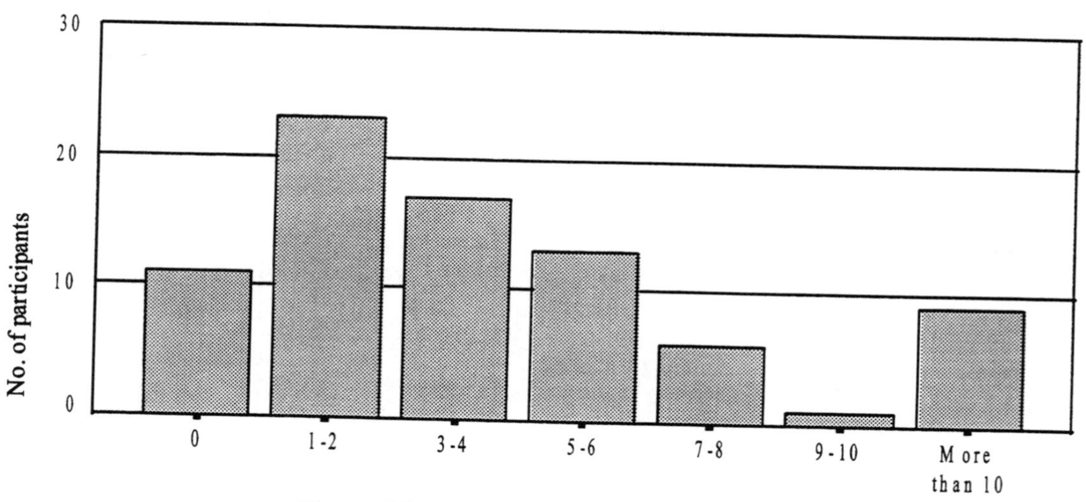

Figure 5.35 – Number of courses attended

Respondents were asked about the support they had received for using ICT in their teaching, other than the training courses that they had attended (see Figure 5.37). The most common form of support was self-help, followed by support from another staff member and the ICT co-ordinator, suggesting that most support was self-support or from other people within the teachers' own institutions. The support for using ICT from professional associations was not mentioned by many, although more than 50% of the sample were not members of any of the three associations considered in this research.

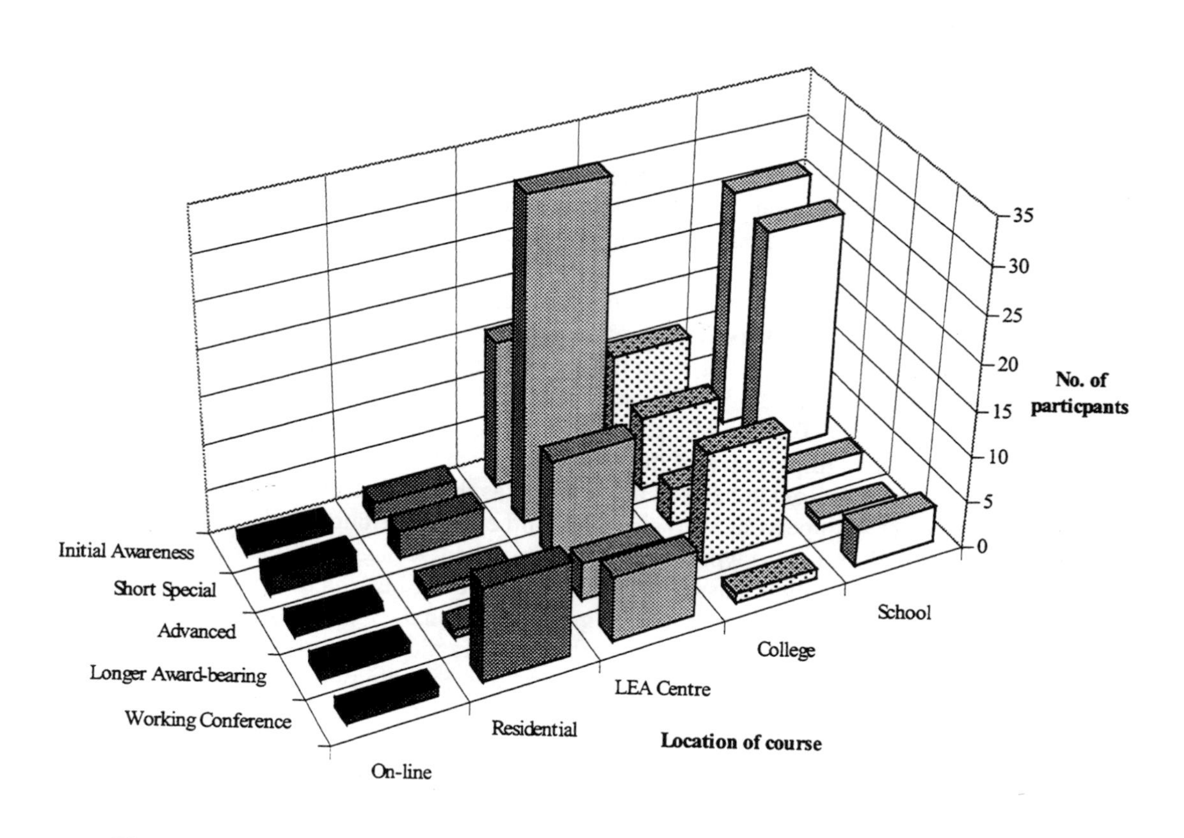

Figure 5.36 – Number of participants who have attended one or more of each form of training course

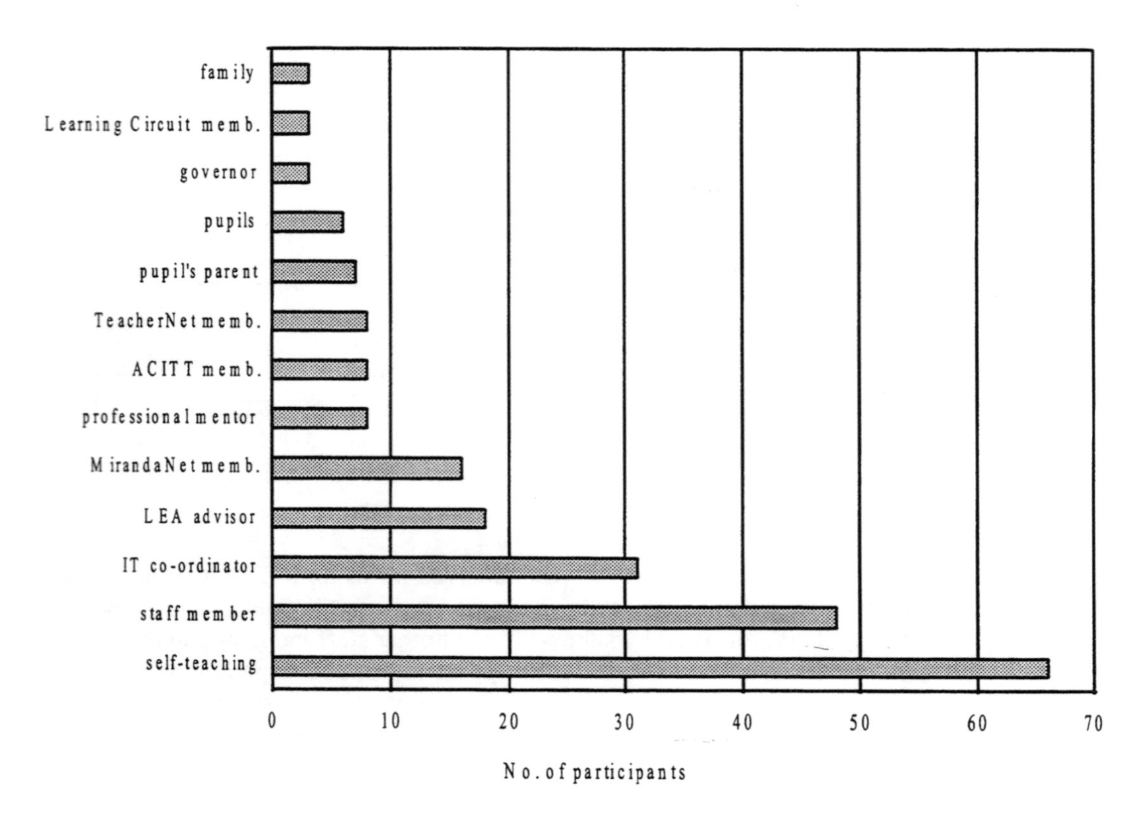

Figure 5.37 – Other forms of support received for using ICT

A number of other forms of support for using ICT that had been received were reported by the teachers, including the National Association of Advisers and Computing Inspectors (NAACE), Research Machines, National Council for Educational Technology (now the British Educational and Communications Technologies Agency, BECTa), the British Computer Society, friends, and other IT professionals.

The teachers were asked the extent to which they agreed that the training they had received had benefited them in various ways. The responses show that the majority agreed that they had experienced all of these benefits, with the exception of changing their classroom practice and understanding the role of the WWW (see Figure 5.38). The most commonly reported benefits were enhanced ICT skills, ideas for using ICT in the classroom and discussion with other professionals. The importance of discussion with other professionals is supported by the views of a MirandaNet fellow, a head of art, who states that "It is of vital importance to be able to talk and meet with persons who can share and even contribute to a vision of educational potential". It is also worth noting that less than 50% agreed that the training they had received had changed their classroom practice. However, lessons using or teaching ICT/IT require a range of practices including good 'traditional' practices as well as innovative teaching methods. Therefore, changing one's teaching practice is not always necessary or beneficial (Cox, 1998). Nevertheless, in order to use the technology that is now available teachers will need to rethink their whole teaching approach due to the new ways in which pupils will be learning.

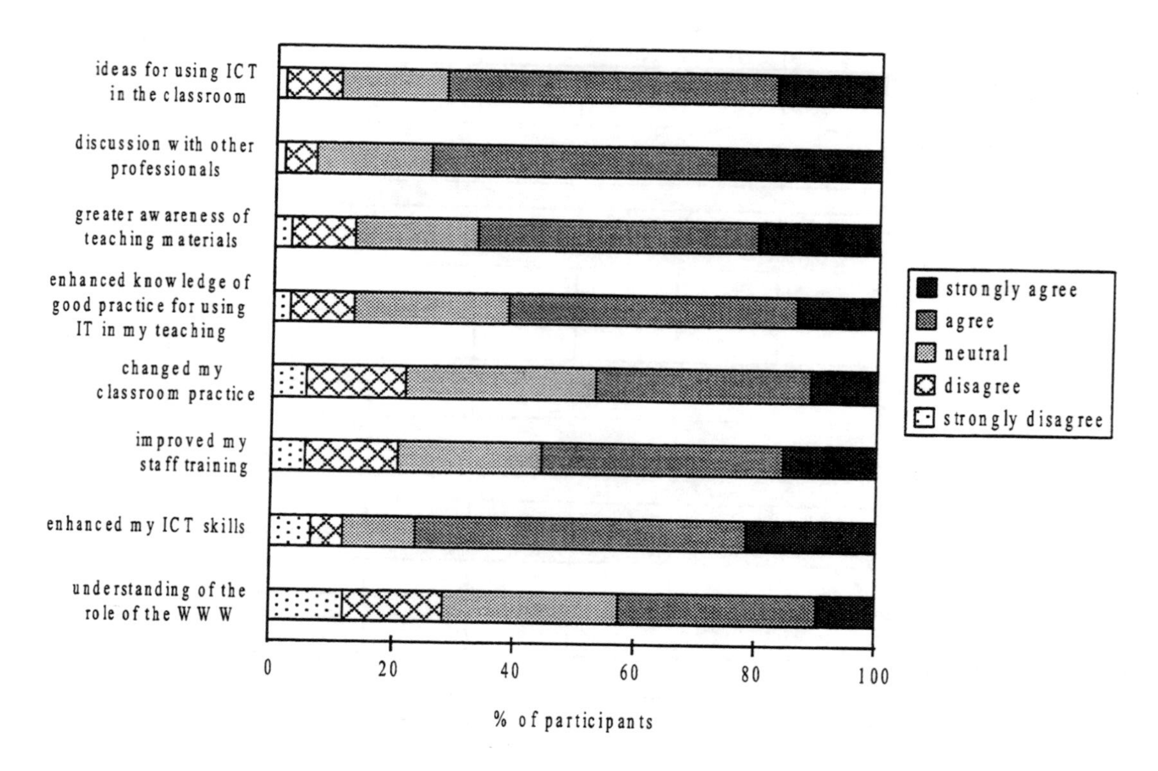

Figure 5.38 – The effects of the in-service training received

Figure 5.39 shows the respondents' perceived value of different forms of training. The three most valued forms of training were ideas for using ICT in the classroom, understanding of how ICT helps learning and advanced ICT skills; all of which are core elements of the New Opportunities Fund training requirements (DfEE, 1998c). The perceived average value of all the forms of training was high, suggesting that many aspects of training are considered to be useful.

The respondents were also asked how they would like training to be delivered, in terms of the location and type of training course. The most popular were short special and initial awareness school courses, with residential courses generally being the least popular (see Figure 5.40). A wide range of courses was chosen indicating the different needs of the teachers.

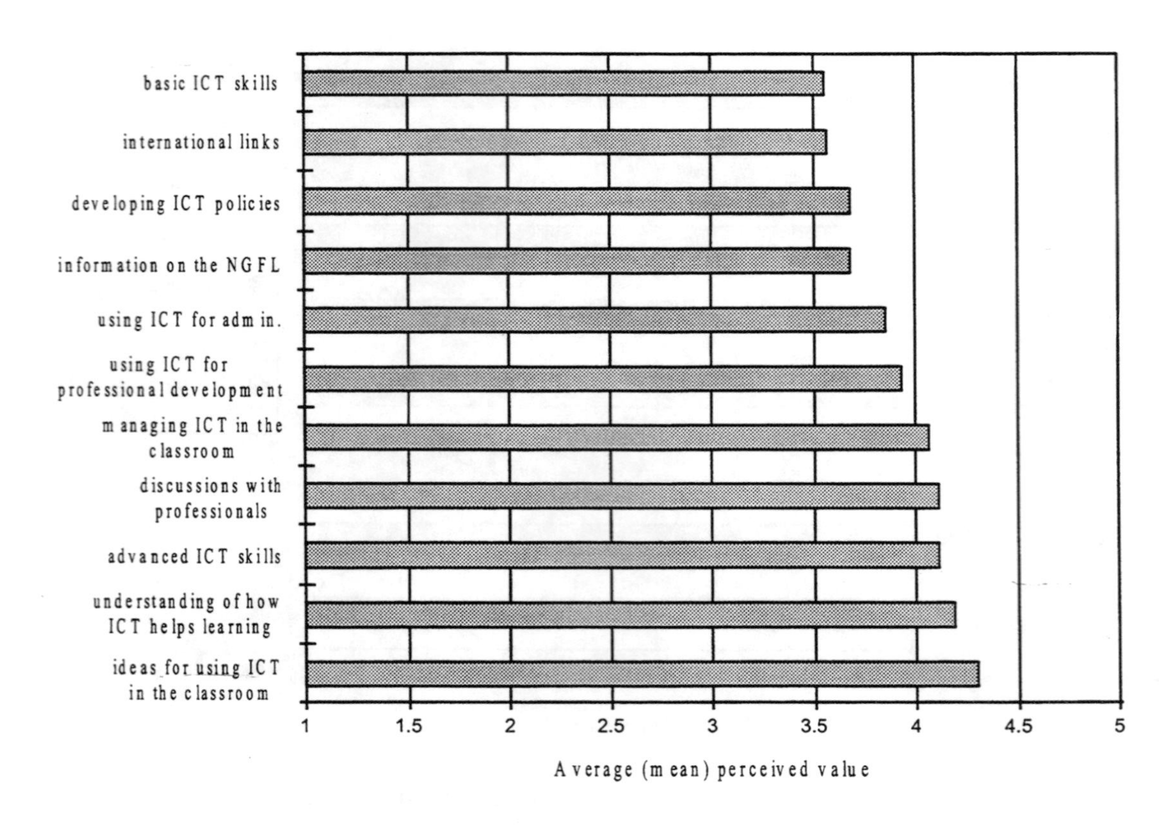

Figure 5.39 – Perceived value of different forms of training

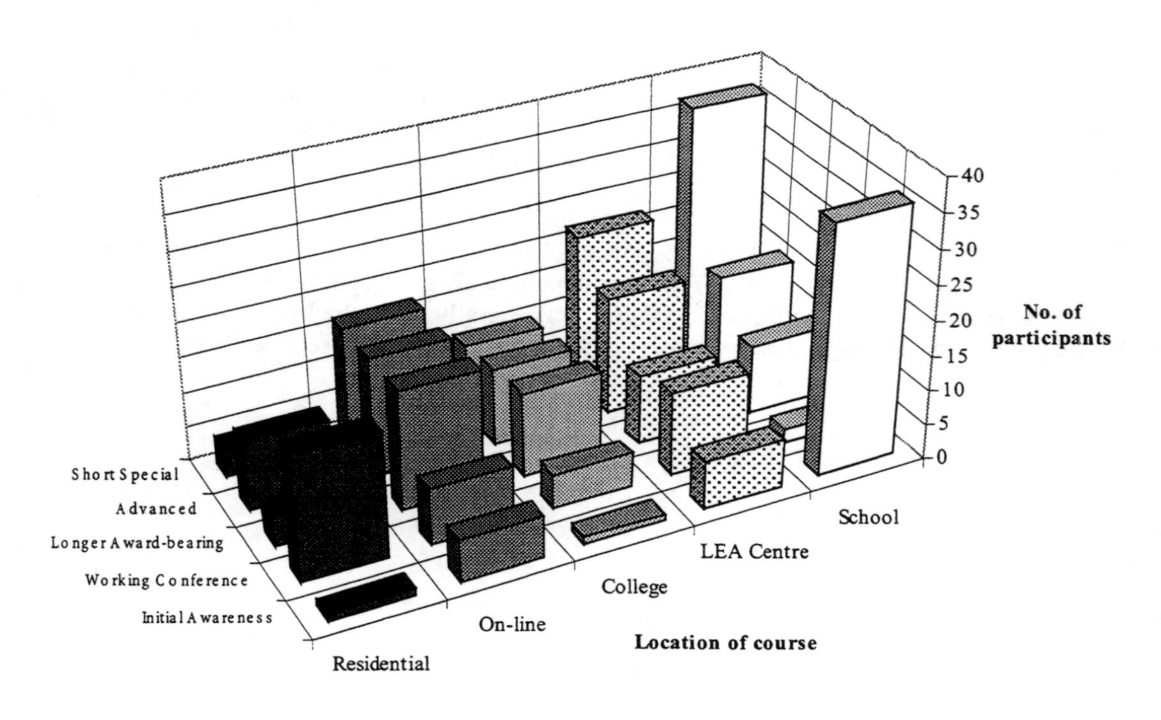

Figure 5.40 – The location and type of training wanted

One of the difficulties reported in earlier research regarding types of training is the reluctance of head teachers to provide supply cover for teachers to attend any out of school courses (Cox and Rhodes, 1990). This is supported by the evidence from the present research, see Figure 5.41, which shows that over 65% believed that funding to attend courses and conferences would enable them to make more use of ICT in their teaching. This suggests that teachers would prefer to attend courses in locations outside school but are mostly unable to do so. Figure 5.41 also shows that many of the ACITT and MirandaNet members who participated in our study responded that they wanted more support from their associations. The vast majority of teachers (72%) reported wanting better resources and a substantial number (34 teachers) consider on-line contact with peers and experts to be beneficial.

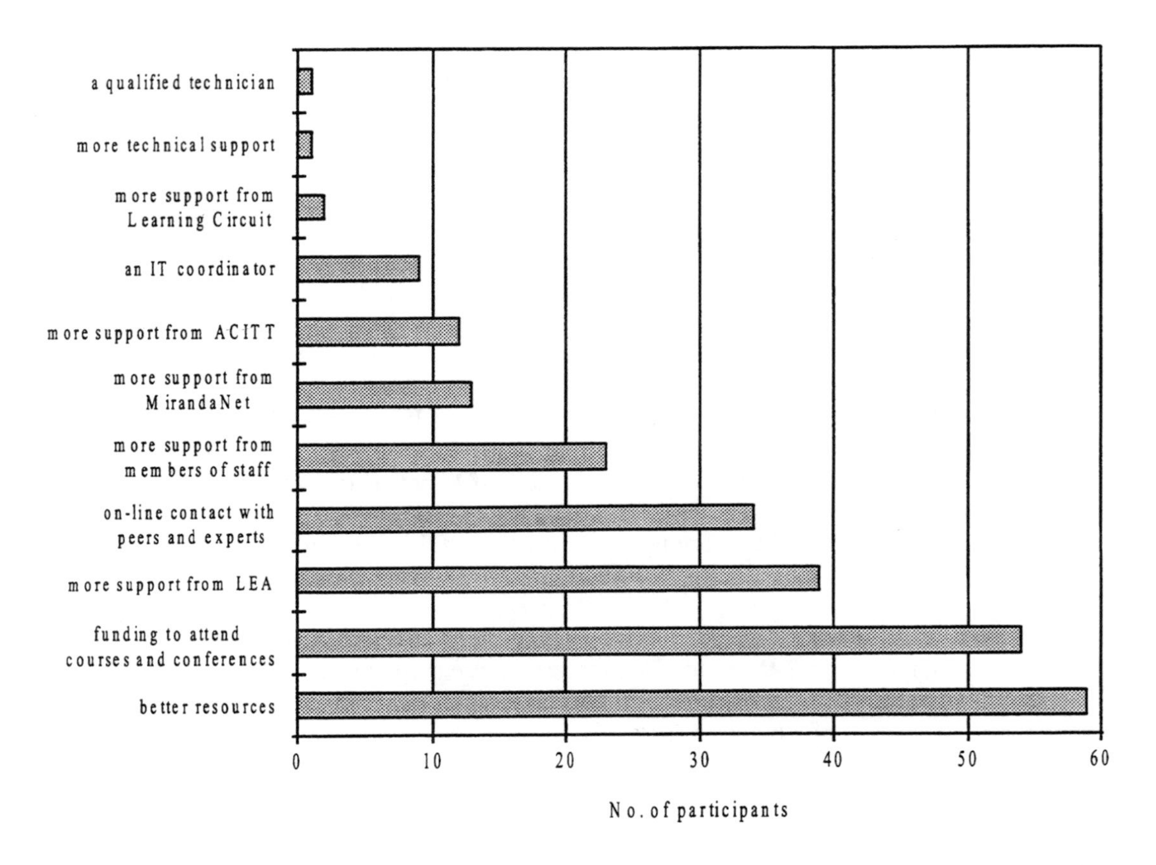

Figure 5.41 – Other support that is perceived to enable the respondents to use ICT more in their teaching

Most of the respondents (78%) had run courses for their colleagues (see Figure 5.42) and a large majority (81.3%) stated that the courses that they had delivered had been successful.

In summary, although some respondents had attended 7 or more courses, the majority had had relatively little ICT training considering the length of time they had been teaching. However, the results show that the teachers perceived the courses that they had attended as having been beneficial in a number of ways. It was clear that the teachers wanted to attend more courses and conferences, and have better resources and support in order to use ICT more in their teaching.

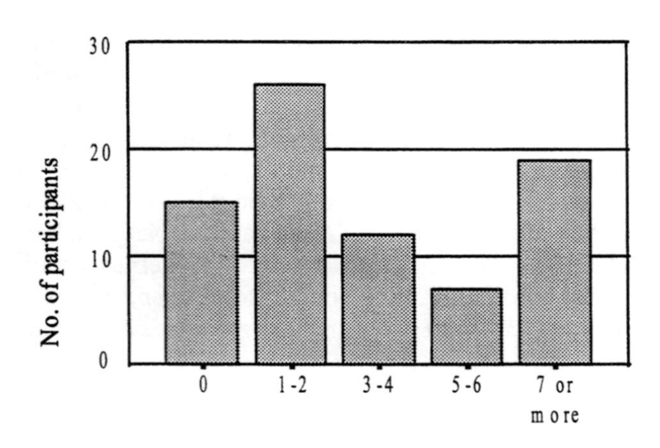

Figure 5.42 – Number of courses delivered

5.8.1 The relationship between training received and use of ICT in school

As one of the main objectives of this research was to investigate the kinds of training courses that can help teachers to use ICT in their teaching, we examined the relationship between the training that the teachers had received and their use of ICT in their teaching. In order to achieve this we compared the results concerning the number of each type of course attended with a score for the use of ICT in teaching. This score was calculated using the participants' responses concerning how frequently they used 11 forms of ICT, including word processing, databases, e-mail and modelling, in their teaching. The educators were asked to estimate how often they used each of these forms of ICT on a scale of 1 (never) to 5 (more than an hour a day). The sum of these responses was then used as the overall score for their use of ICT in teaching. We recognise that this score is only a measure of the frequency of ICT use, not its educational value.

The statistical correlations between types of training received and ICT use in teaching were calculated using a Pearson 2-tailed test and the results are given in Table 5.2. The strength of the relationship is shown by the correlation coefficient, r. The greater r is the stronger the relationship, regardless of whether it is positive or negative. A positive relationship indicates that as one factor increases so does the other, whereas a negative relationship shows that as one factor increases the other decreases. A value of 0 denotes no relationship at all and a value of 1 denotes a perfect relationship. Shaded cells indicate large correlations, i.e. greater than +/-0.3 (for detailed discussion on correlations see Tabachnick and Fidell, 1996).

The results show large correlations between the use of ICT in teaching score and the number of working conferences (r =. 314), and longer award bearing courses (r =. 309) that were attended. In other words, teachers who attended these courses were likely to use ICT more frequently in their teaching. This suggests that, out of the range of courses reported, working conferences and award bearing courses could be the most effective in training teachers to use ICT. This supports the earlier research by Cox and Rhodes (1988), which showed that the most effective training leading to the uptake of ICT by primary school teachers was long award bearing courses rather than short school courses.

Table 5.2 – Correlations between the total number of each type of training course attended and frequency of ICT use in teaching

	Initial awareness courses	**Short special courses**	**Advanced courses**	**Working conf.s**	**Award-bearing courses**	**Freq. of ICT use in teaching**
Initial awareness courses	1.00	0.07	0.14	-0.13	0.18	0.03
Short special courses	0.07	1.00	0.08	-0.10	0.02	-0.06
Advanced courses	0.14	0.08	1.00	0.09	0.34	0.10
Working conf.s	-0.13	-0.10	0.09	1.00	0.11	0.31
Award-bearing courses	0.18	0.02	0.34	0.11	1.00	0.31
Freq. of ICT use in teaching	0.03	-0.06	0.10	0.31	0.31	1.00

5.9 Aspects relating to the membership of professional organisations

This section concerns the responses to the items in the questionnaire about the participants' experiences of the professional organisations to which they belong. A small percentage of the questionnaire respondents belonged to one of the associations, i.e. MirandaNet or ACITT (see Figure 5.2). These participants were asked to complete a small questionnaire, which was an appendix to the main questionnaire, concerning the circumstances of their membership, the services it provides, problems or obstacles limiting the usefulness of the organisations and other services that they would like to receive. Due to the small number of questionnaire respondents who belonged to either of the associations, the results in this section may not be representative of the entire membership.

Of the 14 members of MirandaNet who completed the questionnaire, six heard about MirandaNet through an existing member. The remaining members heard about the fellowship through a conference, the web site, the scholarship, an advert, a letter to their school or a course run by the director. Many of the members joined MirandaNet at a conference and/or were asked to join, and one even joined on line. The majority of the ACITT members who participated in the study heard about ACITT through the BETT exhibition or through conferences, with the remainder hearing about it through a colleague, Microcomputer Users in Schools Education (MUSE, which merged with ACITT in 1991), a mailshot, or King's College London. Again, many joined through a conference. These findings suggest that the most important sources of information about these kinds of associations are word of mouth, the Internet, conferences or mailshots.

Table 5.3 shows that these members of MirandaNet and ACITT had not been members of the organisations for very long. However, it is worth noting that MirandaNet is only 6 years old, although ACITT has been going for 11 years. Furthermore, less than a third (30.8%) of the

ACITT members had been to any ACITT conferences. However, all but one of the MirandaNet members had been to two or more of the MirandaNet meetings.

Table 5.3 – Minimum, maximum and mean length of membership of MirandaNet and ACITT

	Length of membership of MirandaNet (years)	Length of membership of ACITT (years)
No. of members	14	11
Minimum	1	1
Maximum	6	4
Mean	2.14	2.00

Figure 5.43 shows that the majority of the participants who were members of ACITT never communicated with the other members. However, it should be noted that this was a very small sample of the ACITT membership and therefore may not represent the general view. Most of the MirandaNet members communicated with the other members once a week or more, although, again, this was only a small percentage of the membership. Nevertheless, the greater frequency of communication between the MirandaNet members may be due to the focus of this association on on-line communication between teachers as a way of improving professional development, with on-line tutorials, on-line conferencing and web site assignments being a major component of the project. Not all ACITT members have e-mail addresses and as the membership circulation is over 1000, regular e-mail communication amongst members would be overwhelming. However, members can communicate with each other through the ACITT web site. Nevertheless, a finding reported earlier (see Figure 5.27) showing that 61.1% of all the respondents wish to have on-line communication to support their work suggests that this service could be developed more effectively for ACITT members.

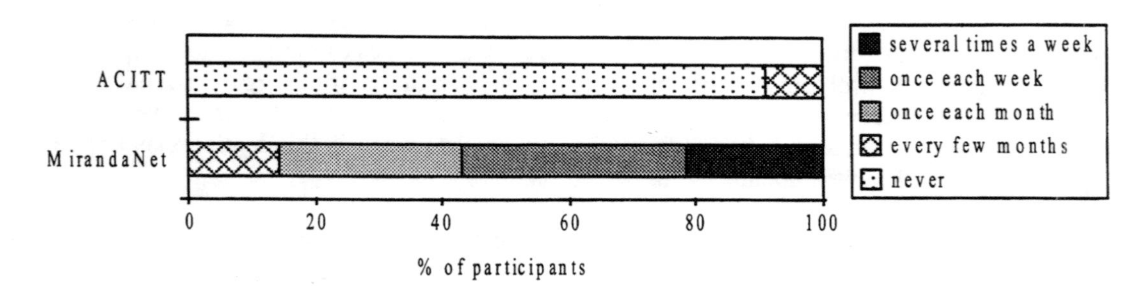

Figure 5.43 – How frequently the members of the two associations communicate with other members of that association

The MirandaNet members who participated in the research gave highly positive responses concerning the benefits of their membership (see Figure 5.44). In particular, the majority agreed that MirandaNet had enabled them to meet like-minded individuals, have greater awareness of the uses of ICT and keep up with advances in ICT. The MirandaNet members were also asked what they considered to be the main advantages of their membership. The responses given included:

- personal development, such as increased confidence in using ICT and public speaking;
- communication and collaboration with other teachers, including international links;

- increased motivation to use ICT effectively;
- better access to resources and research;
- receiving and providing good practice information;
- feeling on the cutting edge of new technology;
- a sense of community.

The other evidence collected from the MirandaNet fellows has also shown how they feel MirandaNet has benefited them:

"The most important aspect of MirandaNet, as far as I am concerned, is to meet people in the same industry and have a chance to exchange ideas and discuss issues. It has been enlightening to visit teachers from abroad and in some ways experience problems and solutions from a different angle. Being able to present reports on what you have done and have a forum for that is useful as it forces one to think carefully about what has happened and reflect on it, as well as pass on information to others" (IT teacher)

"MirandaNet provides an opportunity to disseminate good practice and to share research which is being done in numerous institutions to develop ICT. Through bodies like MirandaNet we can inform, and perhaps influence, policy makers so that the right decisions are made about the development of ICT in education" (Curriculum manager).

"The community of like-minded but disparate individuals is the attraction. We are all banging away at our projects and it is nice to be able to bounce ideas off the other fellows" (Director of an ICT training centre).

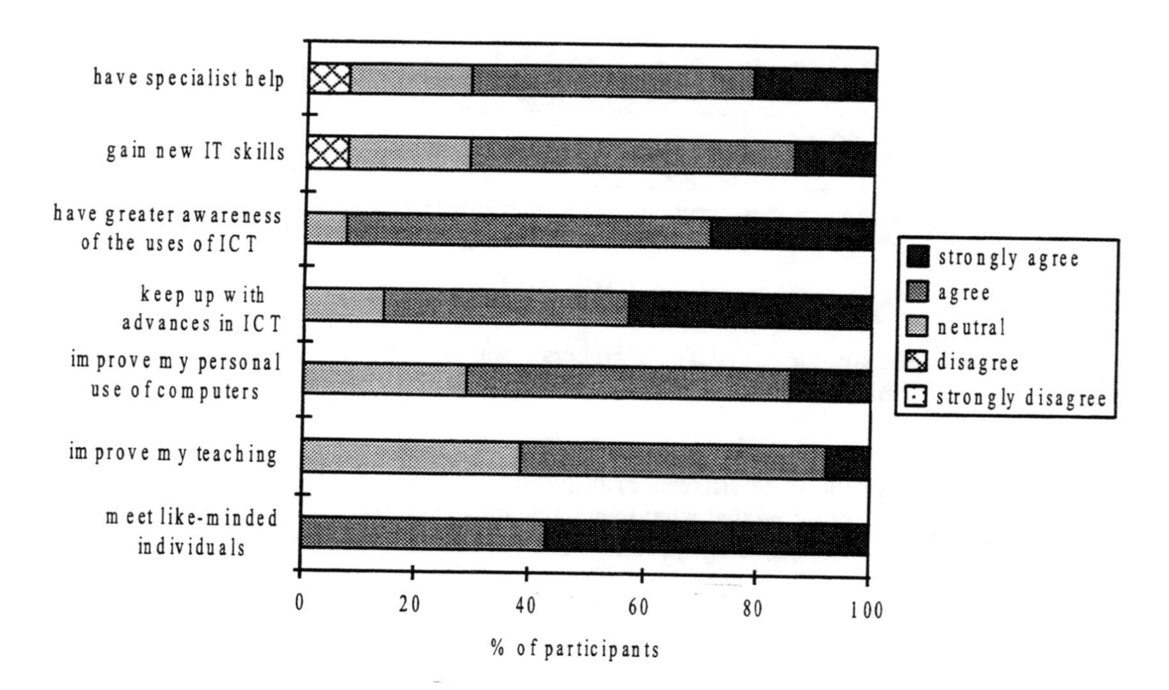

Figure 5.44 – The attitudes of MirandaNet members towards what they have gained from their membership

In comparison to MirandaNet, the members of ACITT responded less positively to the same items concerning the advantages of membership. In particular, generally they did not consider that ACITT enabled them to improve their personal use of computers, gain new ICT skills or improve their teaching. This may be due to the different types of members of the two organisations. For example, the members of ACITT are mainly IT teachers or ICT co-ordinators and so arguably were already highly experienced ICT users in terms of their teaching and personal use. The members of MirandaNet, on the other hand, teach a range of subjects and therefore may have been less proficient in ICT. However, the majority of ACITT members maintained that their membership had enabled them to have greater awareness of the uses of ICT and keep up with advances in IT. Other advantages of ACITT membership that were given included information from the newsletter, being informed of legislation changes and being provided with lesson plans, schemes of work etc.

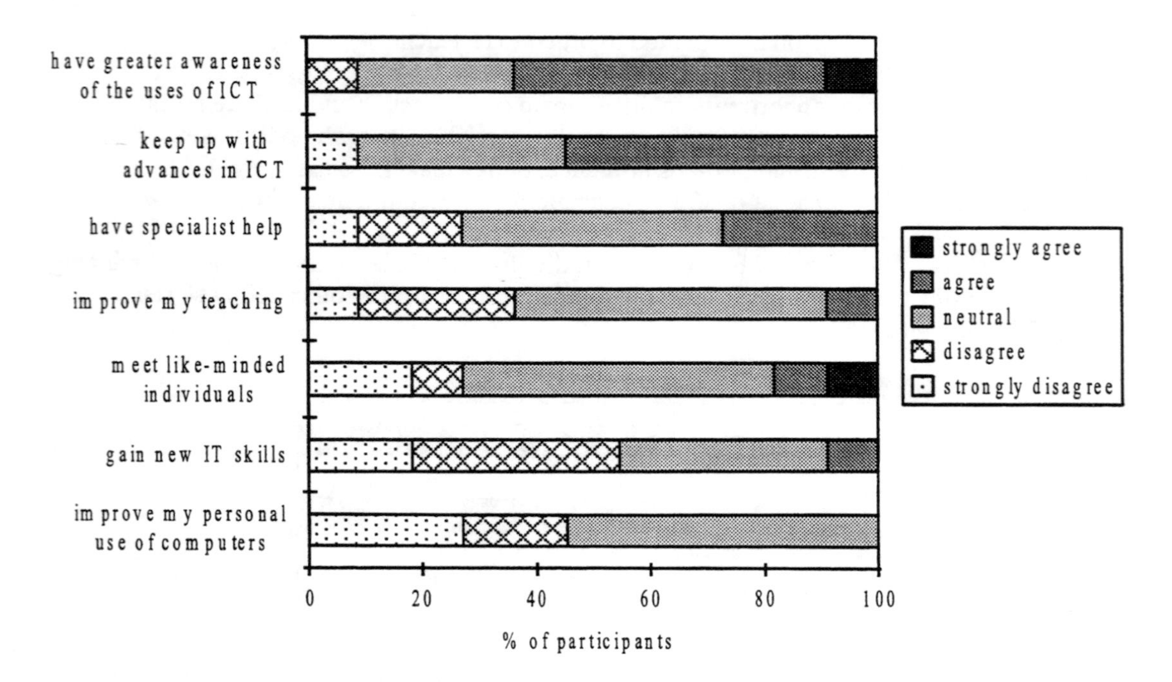

Figure 5.45 – The attitudes of ACITT members towards what they have gained from their membership

Figures 5.46 and 5.47 show the different priorities of the members of the two associations. MirandaNet members reported that what they value most highly are professional activities involving communication with other professionals through conferences and seminars, international exchange, and ideas about funding projects. ACITT members preferred information about new software and hardware, product trials and conferences. Given the different jobs and responsibilities of the members and the small sample sizes, these results are only indicative of the kinds of support that teachers and other educators wanted from their associations. It is clear that they all valued a range of services and help in their professional uses of ICT, which would also be of benefit to those teachers who are not yet members of an ICT in education association.

The members of the two associations were also asked what other services they would like to receive. Members of MirandaNet reported that they would like a list-serve facility to communicate ideas more effectively, more focused grouping of working parties, and sponsorship to enable the respondent's school to develop an Intranet. ACITT members suggested the need for evaluation of products, more schemes of work and ideas for projects, and clearer discussion groups.

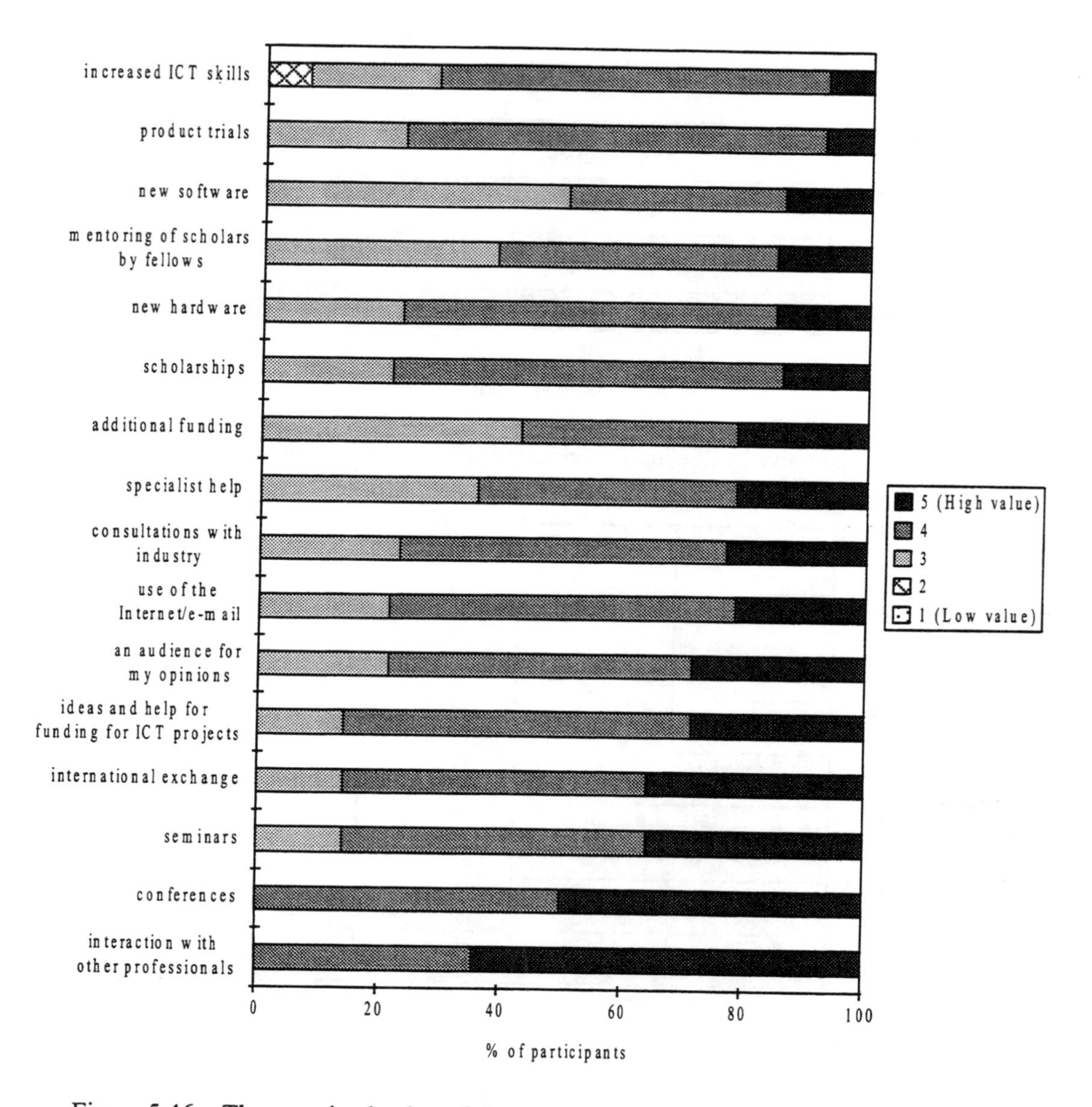

Figure 5.46 – The perceived value of the various services and opportunities offered by MirandaNet

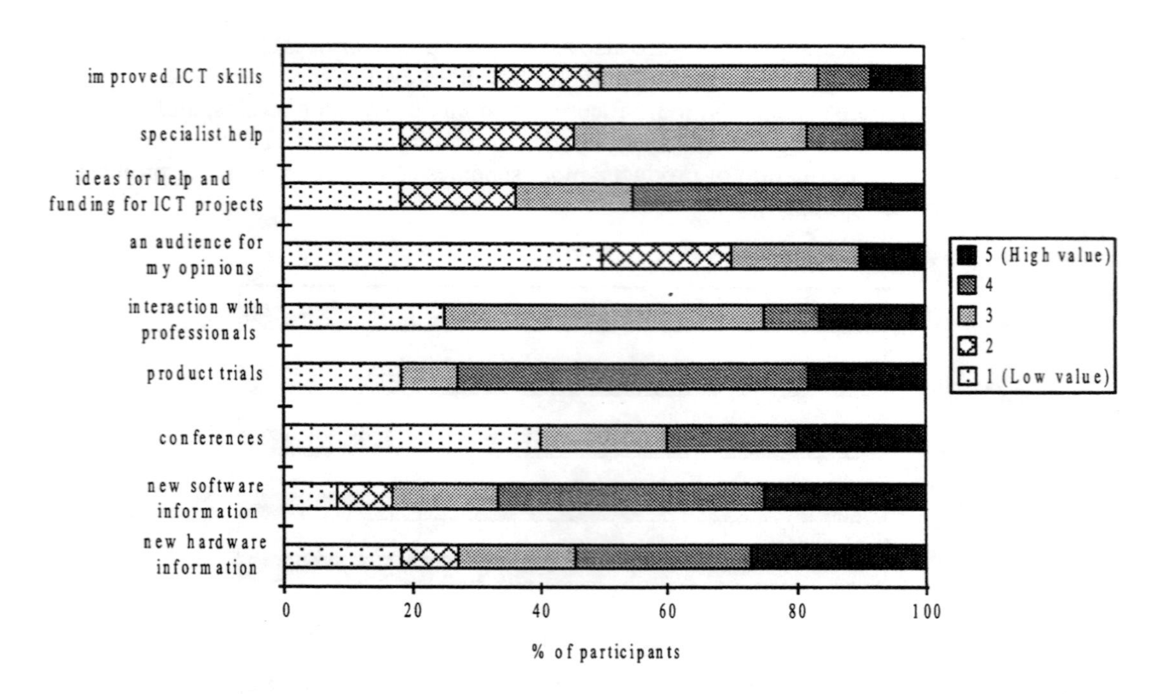

Figure 5.47 – The perceived value of the various services and opportunities offered by ACITT

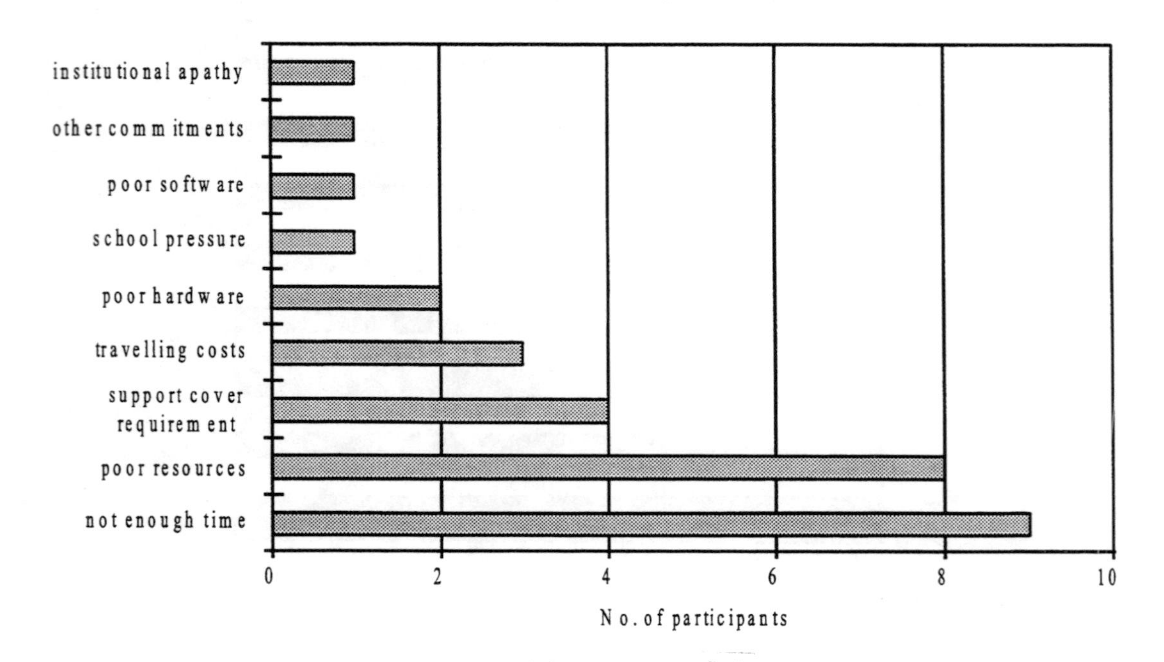

Figure 5.48 – The factors that limit the usefulness of membership of MirandaNet

The most important inhibitor that limited the usefulness of these associations, as shown in Figures 5.48 and 5.49, was "not enough time". Lack of funding was also considered to be a barrier to their membership. This implies that schools should be recognising the value of ICT professional associations and should allocate more time and funding to their staff so they can take full advantage of the services and support that these associations provide.

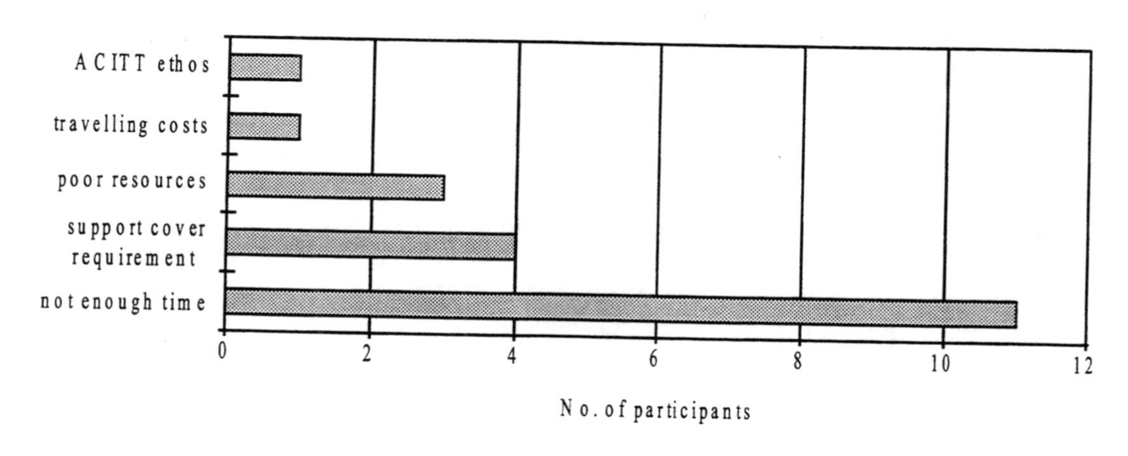

Figure 5.49 – The factors that limit the usefulness of membership of ACITT

Figure 5.50 shows that the members of ACITT and MirandaNet reported wanting to remain active members of these organisations for at least two years, indicating that being a member of a supportive ICT in education association was important to their ICT teaching and use.

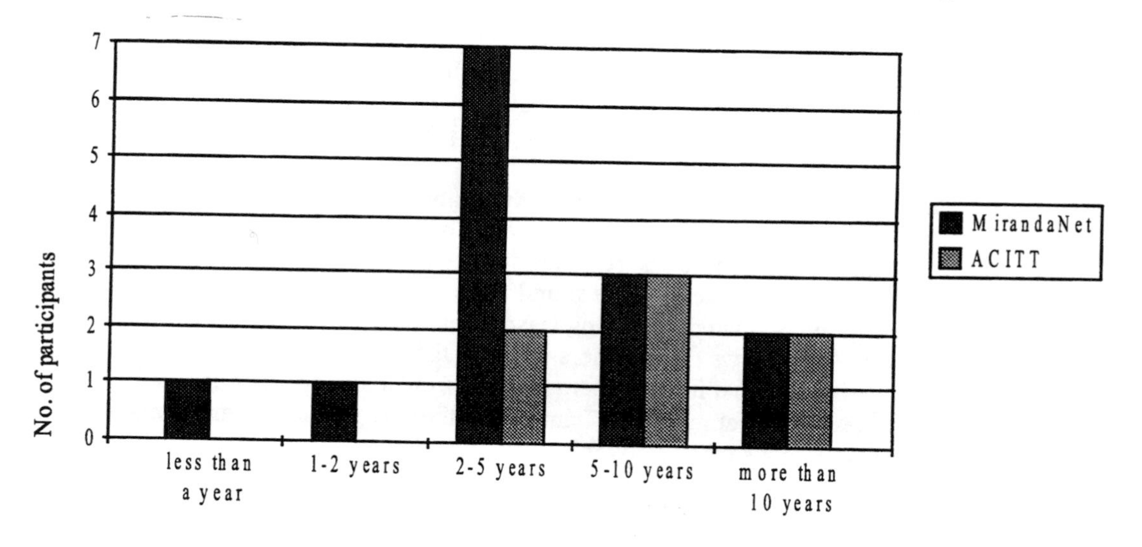

Figure 5.50 – The length of time they want to remain an active member of the associations

ACITT full membership is £30 per year and although MirandaNet membership is currently free, 50% of the MirandaNet members said that they would be willing to continue being a member of MirandaNet if they had to pay a subscription fee. The majority of these participants stated they would not pay more than £30 a year for the subscription.

5.10 Motivating factors

The final analysis stage of the questionnaire results concerns the correlations that were calculated between the different factors comprising ease of use and usefulness, and use of ICT in teaching. These correlations are presented in Appendix A. Large correlations, i.e. those greater than +/-0.3, are highlighted. The higher the number the stronger the relationship, regardless of whether it is a positive or negative value (see section 5.4.1). An example of a strong positive relationship is that between questions 1 and 13. In this case, the large correlation coefficient (r = 0.51) shows that those respondents who find it easy to think of ways of using ICT in their teaching were more likely to feel that using ICT made lessons more interesting for them. There is a strong negative correlation between questions 1 and 3. This shows that those respondents who find it easy to think of ways of using ICT in their teaching were also less likely to have difficulties using software/hardware frequently.

It is worth noting that these findings only show relationships (correlations) between factors and do not demonstrate that one factor affects or causes change in the other. Therefore, with the example stated above, *finding it easy to think of ways of using ICT in lessons* did not necessarily make using ICT more interesting, although this would be one way of interpreting the positive relationship found between these two factors. Some of the relevant relationships that were found between the factors and between these factors and a score of ICT use in teaching (described in section 5.8.1) are discussed in the following sections.

5.10.1 Relationships between the factors relating to perceived ease of use

The correlations discussed above show that there were some strong connections between the perceived ease of use factors. For example, finding it easy to think of ways to use ICT in teaching was negatively related to having difficulties using software and hardware. Therefore, those teachers who experienced difficulties using software/hardware were less likely to find it easy to think of ways of using ICT. In addition, those teachers who found that using ICT makes lessons more time-consuming also tended to be those who felt that it makes preparing for lessons more difficult. Furthermore, those teachers who wanted more time were also more likely to want more staff support and more technical support. These three factors were not affected by the teachers' satisfaction with the level of ICT resources available to them.

5.10.2 Relationships between the factors relating to perceived usefulness

There were strong relationships between most of the factors relating to the perceived usefulness for *teaching*. For example, the responses to the statement that using ICT makes lessons more interesting for the teacher were found to be positively related to making lessons more diverse, and negatively related to making lessons less easy and less fun and restricting the content of lessons. This shows that teachers who felt that using ICT makes lessons more interesting also tended to feel that it made them more diverse, more fun, and less difficult and did not restrict their lessons. Feeling that ICT improved the presentation of materials was associated with finding lessons more enjoyable.

The three factors relating to the perceived usefulness for *pupils*, i.e. feeling that ICT reduced their motivation, impaired their learning, and made lessons more fun, were all strongly related. The findings showed that teachers who felt that using ICT made lessons more fun for pupils were less likely to feel that using ICT impairs pupils' learning or reduces their motivation.

In terms of the benefits for *teachers' professional development or personal use*, there was a very strong relationship between the feeling that using ICT gave them more confidence and that it gave them greater awareness of its uses. This suggests that there is a link between awareness of the uses of ICT and confidence in using it. In addition, teachers who felt that using ICT in their teaching gave them more prestige in school were more likely to feel that it gave them more power in school as well.

The correlations that were calculated also showed some relationships between the three categories of perceived usefulness factors (i.e. usefulness for teachers, pupils, and teachers' professional or personal use) that are worth noting. For example, feeling that using ICT in teaching reduces pupils' motivation was positively related to making lessons more difficult and less fun for the teachers and negatively related to making lessons more diverse and interesting. This indicates that teachers who felt that using ICT improves pupils' motivation also felt that it makes lessons easier for them and more fun, diverse and interesting. In addition, teachers who felt that it enhanced pupils' learning were more likely to find using ICT in their teaching enjoyable.

5.10.3 Relationships between the factors relating to perceived ease of use and perceived usefulness

There were a number of interesting significant relationships between the perceived ease of use and usefulness factors. For example, the results show that those teachers who said that it was easy to think of ways to use ICT in their teaching were more likely to think that ICT made their lessons easier, more interesting, fun, and enjoyable and that it increased pupils' motivation. Furthermore, those teachers who felt that using ICT made preparing for lessons easier were more likely to feel that it enhanced the content of their lessons. Feeling that using ICT made controlling the class more difficult was associated with the belief that it reduces pupils' motivation.

5.10.4 Relationships between motivating factors and use of ICT in teaching

Three of the factors relating to ease of use were found to be related to use of ICT in teaching. Teachers who used ICT more in their teaching were more likely to find it easy to think of ways to use ICT in their teaching, to have less difficulties using software/hardware, and to be satisfied with the resources available. Teachers who used it less in their teaching were also more likely to feel that it was counter-productive due to insufficient resources. In addition, those teachers who wanted to use more educational software in their teaching were more likely to use ICT infrequently in their teaching. This implies that some teachers were motivated to use ICT more but were unable to do so due to insufficient time, inadequate resources, and so on.

Only three of the factors relating to perceived usefulness were found to be significantly related to use of ICT in teaching. The findings showed that teachers who felt that using ICT made lessons more interesting, more enjoyable and easier tended to use ICT more. All these factors relate to perceived usefulness for teaching, indicating that such perceived benefits have a greater motivational effect than those factors relating to perceived usefulness for the pupils or for the teachers' professional development or personal use. These findings suggest that, as shown by previous research (e.g. Watson, 1993), having sufficient resources and finding it easy to use ICT are significant factors relating to ICT use. In addition, our results indicate that three other factors, which have not been widely reported previously, namely feeling that using ICT makes lessons easier, more interesting and more enjoyable for the teacher, are also associated with more frequent use of ICT in teaching.

The strong statistical relationships found between the perceived ease of use factors show that these factors are associated with each other, as was found to be the case for the perceived usefulness factors. This supports the technology acceptance model of Davis, Bagozzi, and Warshaw (1989). However, in contradiction to this model, very few of these factors related to the teachers' use of ICT in their teaching. Despite this, as the vast majority of teachers in our sample reported a high level of ICT use in their teaching this does *not* necessarily imply that these factors were unimportant. Indeed, our study indicates that these factors are associated with extensive use of ICT in teaching because the majority seemed to feel that using ICT was useful in many ways and seemed to find using ICT relatively easy.

6 CONCLUSIONS

The conclusions are based on the results of the questionnaire survey, the analysis of the MirandaNet data and the theoretical and empirical research discussed in sections 2 and 3.

6.1 ICT use at home

94% of the questionnaire sample reported having access to a computer at home and 76% had access to the Internet at home. These findings demonstrate that the majority of respondents had a much higher level of ICT resources for their personal and professional use than the general teaching population, which may suggest that this is a motivating factor for using ICT in teaching. The most popular uses of ICT at home were word-processing, e-mail and desktop publishing.

The educators who completed a questionnaire were asked whether they performed various tasks on their computer at home. Over 90% of the sample could load software, manage files and connect to external devices, and over 75% could format disks, use help facilities, check for viruses, and create sub-directories. This demonstrates that, in general, these teachers had mastered the *basic* ICT skills that are included in the larger set of requirements from the Department of Education and Employment's Initial Teacher Training National Curriculum for the use of ICT within subject teaching (DfEE, 1998c).

6.2 ICT use in teaching

The percentage of teachers that reported using different forms of ICT several hours a week in their teaching were 55% for word-processing, 32% for desktop publishing, 26% for art/graphics software, 24% for spreadsheets, and 24% for e-mail. Other uses included subject specific software and the Internet. The results showed that these teachers were including most themes of the ICT curriculum, i.e. communications, handling information, modelling and simulations and presenting information, although many aspects were only being used once a month.

6.3 Perceived ease of use of ICT

The responses for the items in the questionnaire relating to ease of use suggest that, in general, the teachers felt that ICT was easy to use in their teaching. In particular, very few participants had difficulties using software/hardware, found it difficult to think of ways to use ICT in their teaching or felt that using ICT made it more difficult to control the class. A substantial proportion of teachers did feel, however, that hardware/software problems disrupt lessons and that ICT makes preparing for lessons more time-consuming. In addition, many teachers apparently experienced a lack of support that may have had an impact on their perceived ease of use. The majority of respondents reported that they wanted more technical support and time to use ICT, and many were dissatisfied with the ICT resources available to them. These problems, in addition to the expense, the supervision necessary and a lack of training, were deemed to be the greatest disadvantages of using ICT. In spite of such disadvantages all the teachers in our sample were managing to use ICT in their teaching. The MirandaNet data also demonstrate teachers' need for better training and resources.

6.4 Perceived usefulness of ICT

The most positive responses relating to perceived usefulness were those associated with the benefits for pupils. This is supported by the comments concerning the main advantages of using ICT in teaching. In particular, it was believed that using ICT increases pupils' motivation, makes lessons more enjoyable, aids their learning, increases their interest and concentration, prepares them for the future, and gives them more control over their learning. These findings suggest that the perceived impact on pupils was a major motivating factor for the teachers to use ICT in their teaching. The questionnaire findings also demonstrated that the teachers experienced positive effects on their teaching through their use of ICT. In this respect, the advantages appeared to be increased diversity in teaching activities and the teaching strategies available, and access to better and more diverse resources.

The majority of teachers also felt that using ICT made lessons more enjoyable, interesting, diverse and fun for them. Furthermore, using ICT in their teaching appeared to be beneficial for teachers in other ways, such as allowing them greater access for their personal ICT use, giving them greater awareness of the uses of ICT, increasing their confidence in using ICT and enhancing their career prospects. Therefore, in general, the respondents appeared to find using ICT in their teaching beneficial for a wide range of reasons, suggesting that they used ICT because they perceived it to be useful, rather than because they were obliged to use it due to their professional role, school policy, the national curriculum, pressure from others and so on.

6.5 Value of the Internet

As reported earlier, the vast majority of teachers (76%) had access to the Internet at home, with many teachers also using it at school. However, very few reported that the majority of other staff and pupils at their institution had e-mail addresses at school or at home. The respondents appeared to value the Internet most for accessing professional resources, increasing professional knowledge and skills, and getting advice from experts. In addition, they had visited a wide range of web sites for their personal use, including music, shopping, sport, and travel sites. Many web sites had also been visited for professional reasons. These included those that are associated with their teaching subjects and general education web sites such as the Virtual Teachers' Centre, BBC, RM and BECTa. In 1998/1999 the web sites that were highly valued by these teachers were BBC (37% of participants), TES (18%), Microsoft (16%), and VTC (13%).

6.5.1 NGfL and the provision of e-mail addresses for pupils and staff

Nearly 90% agreed that if all teachers had an e-mail address it would benefit the teaching profession and 60% believed that pupils having e-mail addresses would help them to learn about ICT. The majority of teachers felt that teachers and pupils should be given free e-mail addresses at the same time, as it would enable them to learn together and provide opportunities for all. Just under a third thought that pupils should get them after teachers to enable teachers to develop the necessary skills and confidence to help pupils, to use it effectively in their teaching and to stop teachers feeling threatened or undermined. Very few thought that pupils should get them before teachers or shouldn't get them at all.

A significant minority felt that their institution did not have sufficient resources to take advantage of the NGfL opportunities, although the majority of the teachers said that they and their institution would make substantial use of the NGfL in the future. However, more than 50% did not think that they were well informed about the NGfL. The most valuable sources of information on the NGfL were considered to be the education and educational computing press and on-line investigations, although even these sources were not judged to be highly useful.

6.6 Membership of professional associations

The majority of the 13 members of ACITT who completed our questionnaire never communicated with the other members of this association; most of the 14 MirandaNet members communicated once a week or more with the other members. MirandaNet members were more positive about their institution than ACITT members and in particular felt that MirandaNet had enabled them to meet like-minded individuals, have greater awareness of the uses of ICT, and keep up with advances in ICT. ACITT members agreed with fewer of the statements concerning the advantages of ACITT. Generally, they did not feel that ACITT had enabled them to improve their personal use of computers, gain new ICT skills, or improve their teaching, although this may be due to them having a high level of ICT skills already as the majority are IT teachers or ICT co-ordinators. However, the majority maintained that their membership had enabled them to have greater awareness of the uses of ICT and keep up with advances in ICT. It is worth noting that teachers have varying needs and therefore different teachers may benefit and appreciate support from different associations depending upon their ICT skills and experience, their professional roles, and even their personalities. However, it is recommended that teachers who use ICT should receive social support of some kind due to the dynamic nature of ICT use in general and in education in particular.

6.7 Training and support

With regard to the subjects that the teachers were initially trained to teach, only one teacher out of 82 was initially trained to teach IT. The remainder was mostly trained initially to teach science, humanities or arts. In addition, 11 respondents had attended no in-service training courses; the majority had attended 4 courses or less. The most commonly attended courses had been initial awareness and short special courses based in school or in an LEA centre. Very few had attended on-line courses of any kind. In general it appeared that few had received substantial training in the use of ICT in teaching. Nevertheless, most teachers felt that the training they had received had benefited them in a number of ways. In particular the training had enhanced their ICT skills, provided discussions with other professionals, and given them ideas for using ICT in the classroom. However, less than 50% agreed that the training they had received had changed their classroom practice.

The results showed that the majority of teachers wanted training to be at school in the form of either a short special course (45% of respondents) or an initial awareness course (44%) (respondents were allowed to make more than one choice each). However, it was also shown that those teachers who had attended longer award bearing courses and/or working conferences used ICT more frequently in their teaching. This suggests that opting for short rather than long courses may not be in teachers' best interests regarding integrating ICT into their teaching. The most popular forms of training were ideas for using ICT in the classroom, information on how ICT contributes to children's learning, advanced ICT skills, and discussion with other professionals.

In relation to the other support for using ICT in their teaching that had been received, 86% considered self-teaching to have been an important form of support for using ICT, although teachers need to be motivated to teach themselves. 62% have received support for using ICT from other members of staff and 40% from an ICT co-ordinator. As discussed in section 6.3, many teachers wanted better ICT resources, more technical support and more time to use ICT effectively in their teaching.

The MirandaNet data and questionnaire findings suggest that on-line communities may be particularly useful forms of support for teachers. The reported benefits of MirandaNet include the dissemination of good practice, discussion of issues, collaboration between the members, and personal development. In addition, half of all the participants in our questionnaire survey said that they would be willing to spend about 15 hours a month tutoring colleagues from other institutions through on-line communication; 19% were unsure. A large majority also said that they would like to be a member of a teachers' on-line support network. This indicates that on-line support and professional development was viewed as being beneficial for themselves and other teachers.

6.8 The motivated teacher

The results presented in this report provide useful evidence of what might constitute a 'motivated' teacher with regard to using ICT in teaching. The attributes given here may not apply to all motivated teachers, but are those revealed by our small-scale study.

Motivated teachers believe that ICT makes teaching more enjoyable and interesting for the teacher, as well as for the pupils. They are willing to overcome barriers relating to shortages of resources, technical problems and a lack of technical support. A motivated teacher sees ICT as being easy to use and useful in teaching. He/she is willing to devote personal time and effort to improve his/her skills through self-study and attending courses. Finally, a motivated teacher is keen to extend his/her use of ICT and to share his/her expertise and skills by helping to train others.

6.9 Limitations of the study

We have conducted a small-scale study examining the factors that motivate teachers to use ICT in their teaching. Although, we investigated many factors, including attitudes towards using ICT, personal ICT use and the training and support received, there are a number of factors that, due to the size of our study, we could not consider. These include the influence of other external factors, such as the requirements of the national curriculum, pressures from parents and pupils, schools' ICT policies and development plans, and OFSTED inspection reports. It is likely that these factors will influence teachers' uptake of ICT in their teaching. However, as they will also have an effect on attitudes, these factors would have been measured indirectly in our research.

Much of this report has focused on our respondents as a whole, thus viewing them as a sample of experienced ICT users. Therefore, many of our conclusions are based on viewing their experiences and opinions as being associated with uptake of ICT in schools. We have not compared them with teachers who do not yet use ICT in their teaching. This methodology was chosen specifically to study experienced ICT users so that their motivational experiences could be investigated more fully. Nevertheless, these findings may not be representative of the whole population of teachers who use ICT in their teaching.

6.10 Implications for professional development

The findings of our study demonstrate support for the technology acceptance model of Davis, Bagozzi, and Warshaw (1989). In particular, our sample of experienced ICT users showed that they found ICT to be highly useful and experienced few difficulties in using ICT. Those factors that were found to be relevant to the majority of the teachers were: having access to a computer outside of school and using many different forms of ICT for their personal use; considering ICT to be highly useful, particularly for their teaching and for their pupils; experiencing few difficulties with using ICT; and having attended useful training courses. Although, many of the teachers felt that they had benefited from the training they had received, they wanted to receive more training and also felt that they needed better resources and more technical support and time to use ICT. The teachers in our sample who reported using ICT more frequently in their teaching tended to find it easy to think of ways to use ICT in their teaching, experience fewer difficulties using software/hardware, be more satisfied with the resources available, and feel that using ICT makes lessons easier and more interesting.

The most popular training courses for our sample of experienced ICT users were short special and initial awareness courses. However, the findings suggest that longer award bearing courses and working conferences are associated with a greater uptake of ICT in school. This is also supported by previous research (e.g. Cox and Rhodes, 1988). As many of the respondents reported that more funding to attend courses and conferences would enable them to use ICT more in their teaching, this suggests that teachers may prefer longer courses if they were provided with the money (and time) to attend them.

The findings of our study have many implications concerning the content of training that is necessary to help teachers integrate ICT more effectively into their teaching. It is important to note that teachers value many different forms of training and that the content of training should meet the needs of teachers in accordance with their ICT skills and experience, professional roles, and access to ICT resources. In general, the most valued forms of training for the experienced ICT users in our study were ideas for using ICT in the classroom, greater understanding of how ICT helps learning, advanced ICT skills, and discussion with professionals. However, it is worth noting that inexperienced ICT users may need to learn basic ICT skills as well. These findings suggest that teachers do not just want to learn how to use the technology, but also want to know how it can be used most effectively to teach their pupils. It is unlikely that these forms of training could be integrated into short courses for teachers, indicating that longer training courses would be more beneficial.

In addition to these aspects of training, our findings show that teachers who use ICT in their teaching on a regular basis found ICT relatively easy to use and found ICT to be useful to them, their teaching, and their pupils. Therefore, training programmes for inexperienced ICT users should attempt to address teachers' perceptions concerning ease of use and usefulness. Enhancing teachers' perceived ease of use may be achieved by improving their ICT skills, increasing their confidence, and by providing them with adequate resources, sufficient time, and technical and social support. It is even more essential that teachers' perceptions concerning the benefits of ICT are improved. In particular, training programmes should focus on the advantages of using ICT for pupils' motivation, learning, and interest in lessons. Teachers should also be encouraged to view ICT as making their lessons easier, more interesting and more diverse, and be shown how ICT can improve the presentation of their materials and broaden the content of their lessons. Finally, teachers may use ICT more in their lessons if they believe it will give them greater access to computers for their personal use, give them more confidence in using ICT and enhance their career prospects.

Many of the teachers felt that they would like more technical support and time and better resources. These findings and previous research suggest that it is essential that teachers are provided with these forms of support to enable them to use ICT effectively in their teaching. This is particularly important at present due to the pressure on teachers to adopt new technologies from parents, pupils, the government and so on. Furthermore, teachers may benefit significantly from having access to ICT resources outside of school in order to develop their ICT skills, become more aware of the uses of ICT, and encourage them to use ICT for personal and professional reasons. The government is taking some steps towards providing support through the used computers scheme, a subsidised computer for every teacher and low cost on-line resources (e.g. National Grid for Learning and Virtual Teachers' Centre).

Another form of support that may enable teachers to use ICT more is membership of professional ICT in education associations, as indicated by the findings relating to MirandaNet and ACITT. These associations have been found to benefit teachers by providing them with greater awareness of the uses of ICT and allowing them to keep up with advances in ICT and to meet like-minded individuals. The development of a learning community also appears to be highly valuable, as teachers can disseminate good practice, communicate and collaborate with other teachers and become more motivated to use ICT.

PROFESSIONAL DEVELOPMENT FRAMEWORK

> "There are teachers who use ICT in a confident and innovative way on a regular basis. However, for others, ICT remains something they are not sure how to use properly in the classroom. This NOF initiative will help all that change by making high quality training available to all teachers and school librarians who need it." (New Opportunities Fund, 1999)

Introduction to the framework

The aim of the New Opportunities Fund (NOF) training programme is to provide all teachers with access to high quality training and training materials over the next three years, with the core objective of all teachers being confident and competent in making decisions about when, when not and how to use ICT effectively within their subject teaching. However, this initiative begs two very important questions:

1. How effective will the training be in encouraging the *actual* use of ICT in the curriculum?
2. What constitutes *effective* training for the individual teacher?

Neither question is new or unexpected. A study by Ridgway and Passey in 1991 showed that many teachers viewed their INSET training as being useful and as having made them more convinced of the use of ICT in teaching. However, only a small number of these teachers reported having utilised the training to develop the use of ICT in their lessons. Based on their findings, the authors argued that in order for training to be effective it should maintain a constant focus upon classroom practice, take into account the radical effects that ICT can have upon the teaching environment, and address progression in staff skills. Furthermore, they claimed that training courses need to involve consultation, negotiation and communication within school and be an integral part of other school management plans, policies and strategies. When properly implemented, the NOF ICT training initiative should cover all these points, but nevertheless they should still be brought to the attention of colleagues who have the task of co-ordinating this initiative within their schools.

The results of our research support Ridgway and Passey's findings: for the majority of the teachers in our sample, the training that they had received had not changed their classroom practice. Furthermore, the findings of our questionnaire survey and other evidence collected demonstrates the need for training to focus on changing classroom practice, professional and personal development for teachers, and support from other members of staff and senior management. However, our research also indicated that there are a number of other elements that need to be included in training programmes in order to motivate teachers to use ICT in their teaching. These elements, in addition to other aspects of training that have been shown to be important by previous research, were used to create the professional development framework for teachers that is presented here.

One outcome of our research project was to develop a framework for in-service education, linking teacher education strategies to motivation. In particular, we wanted to provide teachers and teacher educators with some basic guidelines for supporting and encouraging teachers to integrate ICT into their teaching. A provisional framework was developed using the findings from our questionnaire survey and the other materials from MirandaNet, various publications and the experience of the authors in the field of education and teacher training.

The main focus of the framework is on training courses, although it is important to note that teachers also need other forms of support in order to be able to use ICT effectively in their teaching, such as adequate ICT resources, help from professional associations, appropriate school policies and so on. We also note that there are new techniques for the professional development of teachers, which include mentoring on line and building on-line learning communities. Some universities, such as the Open University, already have extensive knowledge of running courses on line, yet schools are still in the earlier stages of training their teachers on line. The introduction of new software environments, such as IBM's Lotus Learning Space, Soft Arc's First Class and Oracle's Think.com, offer powerful learning environments and facilities to develop on-line learning communities. However, the teaching profession will need to develop the teaching and moderating skills that are required to use these facilities effectively.

The framework has been designed to offer general guidelines concerning the most effective elements of training that can motivate teachers but also to take account of the different needs and situations of teachers and the implications that they have for training. The provisional framework that was developed in 1999 was discussed at a focus group meeting with practitioners in the field.

Twenty educators attended the focus group meeting, which was held on March 16th 1999. The attendees included ICT co-ordinators and IT and other class teachers from both primary and secondary schools, most of whom were MirandaNet and ACITT members who had responded to the questionnaire. The remaining participants were ICT in education specialists from universities and the Teacher Trainer Agency. For the first part of the meeting, there was a presentation on the background, methodology, and significant findings of the present study. The second part involved a presentation of the key issues of professional development for teachers. The attendees were then divided into three groups in order to discuss the current professional development opportunities available to teachers and the provisional framework. The educators were asked to give their views concerning the implications of the study's findings for training, the kinds of support and training that they believed would benefit teachers and help them to use ICT effectively in their teaching, and their thoughts on the issues that should be included in the framework. The findings of the focus group meeting were utilised to develop the framework further.

It must be stressed that this is a dynamic framework in the process of development and that it will be updated in accordance with new research and responses from teachers and teacher educators. It is published on the Internet (www.compaq.co.uk/education), and is therefore available to schools, LEAs, professional associations, and other workers in the field of education. Finally, a further focus group meeting is planned to discuss new issues and to refine the framework.

The Framework

This framework offers guidelines for teachers, senior managers and teacher educators to help them to choose an effective training strategy. It provides advice concerning the forms of training and support that will help teachers to integrate ICT into their teaching by increasing their motivation. It also details the differences between teachers that will have implications for the form of training that they will find most useful. However, there are no hard and fast rules. The training needs of the staff in any given institution need to be assessed, taking these factors into account, in order to decide which is the right training approach.

To help teachers and teacher educators develop a clearer idea of teachers' training needs we have drawn up a **chart of the factors that need to be taken into account when choosing a training strategy**. For ease of use we have divided these factors into three broad headings: Inputs, Processes, and Outputs.

> The **Inputs** reflect the status quo relating to the trainees and their school, indicating the factors that will affect the form of training that is needed: the trainees' professions, their ICT skills and knowledge, the resources that are available, etc.
>
> The **Processes** reflect the nature, location and content of the training, and other supporting activities and materials that will help teachers integrate ICT into their teaching.
>
> The **Outputs** reflect the goals of the training, and how its effectiveness could be assessed.

Whilst the categories in each section are not meant to be mutually exclusive, it is clearly advantageous to make sure that the training provided matches the teachers' requirements in as many of the sections as possible. If training is to be delivered to several teachers, it may be possible to compromise on some areas, but if the needs of different members of staff are radically different, group training is unlikely to be successful.

In order to make decisions about the training strategy that is appropriate, trainees can work through the different categories, either individually or in a group, identifying their training needs by taking account of the trainee factors and school context. The results can then be used to decide the kind of training that is needed. This will also help schools decide which training provider can best meet these needs.

A. Trainee factors

Professional role

Clearly the form of training that educators will require will depend upon their position and responsibilities within the school. For example, ICT co-ordinators may need training concerning advanced ICT skills, the uses of ICT in different subject areas, how to help other teachers use ICT, and so on. Senior managers may benefit from courses involving basic ICT skills, advice on how to develop an ICT policy for their school, ideas and help for getting funding, and information on the types of software and hardware that are available.

On the other hand, subject teachers will need to be taught how to integrate ICT into their subject curriculum, how to manage ICT in the classroom, and how ICT contributes to pupils' learning. IT teachers, librarians, administrators, advisors, and teacher educators will also have different training needs. There will, however, be some overlap concerning the types of training that different staff will find useful. **Some forms of training will benefit all educators, such as basic or advanced ICT skills, the contribution of ICT to pupils' learning, use of ICT for administrative and personal purposes, and information on the benefits of using ICT**.

Level of ICT experience/knowledge

In most schools, the staff will differ greatly in terms of their ICT knowledge and skills. Indeed, there are still many teachers who have a very low level of ICT skills or none at all. Clearly, before they can use ICT in their teaching, these teachers will need to be taught basic ICT skills. At the other end of the scale, teachers who already use educational ICT, may value working conferences or advanced courses, to discuss issues with other professionals, obtain information on new technologies, and develop new ideas for using ICT in the classroom. The training needs of the trainees in relation to their ICT skills can be assessed using a CD-ROM that has been produced by the Teacher Training Agency (1999). **It is vital that the form of training that is provided is suited to the trainee's level of expertise, in order to avoid experienced teachers becoming bored or frustrated, or frightening off novice users.**

B. School Context

Level of ICT resources available

The training provided should, as much as possible, be appropriate for the level of ICT resources that teachers have access to at present, or will be likely to have access to in the near future, both at home and at school. There is no point training teachers to use Office 2000 when they only have access to Office 95 or training teachers to use an interactive whiteboard if they will not have access to one for another five years. Previous research has shown that teachers involved in a training programme need to be able to assimilate what they have learnt back in the classroom during the training period. Consequently, training courses for relatively inexperienced users may be most effective if they involve the equipment that the teachers are familiar with and have access to.

The teachers' (and their pupils') **access to the resources** must also be taken into account. Our research indicates that insufficient access to ICT equipment can be a major barrier to ICT use. In many schools, teachers may only be able to use ICT in their lessons a few times a week and may have little access for non-teaching purposes. In such cases, they may have little time to use ICT to prepare materials for their lessons, nor to be able to set their pupils tasks requiring substantial ICT use, etc.

However, teachers who have frequent access to high level resources at home and at school, may benefit from training on how to use e-mail in their teaching, how to access resources on the Internet, how to use sophisticated forms of ICT, such as video conferencing, and so on. Clearly, these forms of training would be of little use to teachers with a lower level of resources.

ICT delivery strategy

A major factor that will influence the way in which ICT is used in schools is whether or not ICT is being taught as a separate subject or within other subjects or both. Before the publication of the new English national curriculum it was not compulsory for teachers to use ICT in their teaching, although it was a requirement that all pupils were taught IT. The revised national curriculum produced in January 2000 requires all teachers to use ICT in their teaching. This will have a large impact on how ICT is delivered in schools, how the resources are shared out and who gets training as a priority.

Previous OFSTED reports and other research have shown that pupils learn IT more effectively in schools where it is taught as a separate subject. This is not surprising because learning IT is like learning English, i.e. although English is used in all subjects, a significant amount of time-tabled teaching of English needs to be conducted in order to fulfil the national curriculum requirements.

Training programmes need to take account of how ICT is delivered in schools, who has the most urgent need, how different levels of skills and knowledge can be addressed, and how different subject teachers' training needs can be met. It is clear from our research and other studies that within any single school there is a wide range of training needs, yet there are still single INSET days being held all over the country for ICT awareness and training. These single INSET days may be a way of first introducing the value of ICT to teaching and learning but they have little impact on teachers' professional uses of ICT in their teaching.

School management style

Our research has shown that the delivery of ICT and its use in other subjects is managed differently from school to school. Some schools assign the responsibility to an ICT co-ordinator, other schools to the head or deputy head, and in the case of many primary schools, this might be an additional responsibility for another subject teacher or a head of year. The way the school organises its management and delivery of ICT will affect the ability of the school to promote ICT use in all subjects and will also require different approaches to training.

At present, many schools still assign this responsibility to an ICT co-ordinator, who is expected to teach all the pupils the ICT/IT curriculum and to help all the other teachers in the school to use ICT in their subjects as well. When schools rely too heavily upon one person to fulfil all these roles it is unlikely that this person will have the time to help co-ordinate substantial training as well. **In order for the new training initiatives to be effective, many schools will have to rethink their ICT management procedures and will need to think seriously about improving their ICT staffing levels**. This will be necessary for ICT teaching and use to be effectively integrated into these institutions and for the teachers to be provided with the training that is required.

C. Nature of training

Our study of teachers who were experienced users of ICT, and had attended a wide variety of courses, indicated that some forms of training are particularly valuable. These were:

- school-based training using their own equipment in the environment in which they will be using ICT;
- initial awareness courses to get to grips with the technology;
- short courses with manageable time-spans;
- longer courses for teachers who have achieved a basic understanding of ICT and its uses, covering a number of issues, such as innovative ways of using ICT in the classroom, theories of how ICT contributes to pupils' learning, advanced ICT skills etc.

Despite the fact that initial and awareness courses were the most popular forms of training, our study and previous research suggest that **longer courses are more likely to lead to more frequent use of ICT in teaching**.

There are many different forms of training available, ranging from classroom style courses and seminars to distance learning through books, the Internet, or CD-ROMs. Training may also involve one or more of the following: lectures, hands on sessions, group discussions, individual learning, mentoring etc.

The NOF training, which places an emphasis on distance learning and self study, has not been in progress long enough for us to know how effective distance learning is for teachers' ICT use in the classroom. However, the positive support for on-line communities revealed in our study does show that a distance learning component may be of value to some, if not all, teachers, although our results are not conclusive, as few respondents had yet had the opportunity to experience the support of an on-line community.

The type of training that will be useful to a particular group of teachers will depend upon the preferences of the trainees and providers and other factors such as the desired content of training, the number of trainees, their expertise, cost of the training and so on.

D. Supporting activities and materials

In order to help teachers to use ICT in their teaching, there are a range of supporting activities and materials that training programmes can provide, including:

- information on software and hardware available;
- opportunities to discuss issues with others;
- lesson plans and schemes of work;
- ideas and help for obtaining funding;
- follow up activities, such as on-line help and handouts.

Although training courses can provide teachers with essential ICT skills and an understanding of the uses of ICT and how to integrate it into their teaching, due to the dynamic nature of ICT, teachers will need on-going professional support after the course has finished. This can be achieved through membership of an ICT in education association, support of an ICT co-ordinator or other members of staff, attendance at working conferences and so on.

The findings of our study have shown that on-line communication with other teachers and experts is highly valued by teachers who are experienced ICT users. Members of on-line learning communities can benefit from:

- dissemination of good practice;
- personal development, such as increased confidence in using ICT and public speaking;
- communication and collaboration with other teachers;
- increased motivation to use ICT effectively;
- better access to resources and research;
- improved ability to write educational materials for the World Wide Web;
- greater understanding of the culture of the World Wide Web;
- a sense of community and collegiality.

The Internet provides a new way for teachers to share the skills and expertise that they have acquired through training. This could involve publishing lesson plans, schemes of work, curricula materials and reports on action research studies that they have conducted. Through this process, they can obtain feedback on their expertise and knowledge from a wider community of fellow teachers. Educational debates and other on-line community discussions are often helpful to participating and other teachers. There are examples of group learning materials published on the web sites of MirandaNet and other organisations (see useful contacts and web sites listed at the end of this report).

E. Focus of training

The content of the training should, as much as possible, address the needs of the teachers, in accordance with the factors discussed above. In order for teachers to use ICT effectively in their teaching, it is essential that they have acquired certain knowledge, skills, and teaching strategies, and the **motivation** to put these into practice in the classroom. Therefore, training programmes for inexperienced users of ICT should attempt to cover as many of these aspects as possible. Although individual training courses may not be able to provide all of them, teachers should be given additional support and be encouraged to learn some skills on their own. The elements of training programmes that will help teachers to integrate ICT effectively into their teaching are outlined below, although it is worth noting that experienced users may have received training in some of these areas already.

Basic ICT skills
There is a need for **skills-based** training. The NOF-based training does not address this issue, and instead assumes a certain level of ICT competence. The teachers in our study, who used ICT on a regular basis, had spent a great deal of time gaining and enhancing their ICT skills. One may fairly conclude from this that lack of expertise will be a major barrier to classroom use.

The skills required may be quite basic, but are nevertheless important. They include

- loading software;
- file management;
- virus checking;
- formatting disks;
- accessing help facilities;
- connecting to external devices (printers, modems, scanners etc.).

The NOF training requirements intentionally exclude this level of training, and therefore for non and novice ICT users it will need to be provided elsewhere, ideally prior to receiving NOF training.

Advanced ICT skills
Although the teachers in our study reported using a wide range of forms of ICT, they actually spent most of their time using word-processing software. Training is therefore needed in all areas, to counter this reliance on relatively low-level word-processing skills. Teachers should be taught and encouraged to use a wide range of ICT facilities, including spreadsheets, desktop publishing, WWW and e-mail as well as advanced word processing tools for creating tables, importing pictures and graphs etc. However, the main focus of ICT skills training should be on developing teachers' abilities to use ICT for various purposes, including:

- communicating information;
- handling information;
- modelling;
- interpreting information;
- simulating physical processes.

These are all components of the English national curriculum for ICT.

Use of ICT in teaching and learning
The teachers in our study reported that the courses that they had attended had enhanced their ICT skills, provided discussions with other professionals and had given them ideas for using ICT in the classroom. However, less than half said that the training had led to a change in their classroom practice. **There is a need for all training to be related to practice**.

Furthermore, using ICT for teaching often involves very different teaching methods from those used in traditional practices. Therefore, teachers also need to be helped to **develop appropriate pedagogical practices**. In particular, teachers need training concerning:

- how to fit ICT into the subject curriculum;
- how to combine ICT with other activities;
- ideas for using ICT in the classroom;
- information on how ICT contributes to children's learning;
- accommodating the different abilities of pupils and the pace at which they learn;
- developing progression in pupils' learning;
- how to assess pupils' ICT knowledge and skills;
- how to assess pupils' achievements in subjects when using ICT.

The specific subject needs, particularly of secondary teachers, should be addressed by trainers. There is a pressing need for training in the use of **subject-specific software**, and the teachers reported a strongly felt desire to use more of this in their lessons. In particular, teachers should be taught how to use various forms of ICT to teach their subjects, including measurement and control, interface software and equipment, simulations and role-playing.

Improved motivation by emphasising the advantages of using ICT
It is clear that teachers will not integrate ICT effectively into their teaching unless they are motivated to do so. One of the most effective ways of motivating teachers, as indicated by our research, is to enhance teachers' **perceptions of the usefulness of ICT**. In particular, training should demonstrate the advantages of using ICT in teaching for:

- pupils, by increasing their motivation, enhancing their learning, increasing their interest, enjoyment and concentration, giving them greater control over their learning, and developing the ICT skills necessary for their future careers;
- teachers' educational work, by improving pedagogical practices through an increased diversity in teaching activities and strategies, providing access to better and more diverse resources, and making lessons more enjoyable, interesting, diverse and fun for the teachers;
- teachers' personal and professional development, by promoting a greater awareness of the uses of ICT for personal and administration purposes, increasing confidence in using ICT, and enhancing career prospects.

Improved motivation by developing strategies to overcome barriers to using ICT
Using ICT can often be difficult, especially for those who lack the necessary skills or knowledge. Therefore, teachers need to be shown how to overcome barriers to using ICT in their teaching. In particular, teachers should be taught how to:

- manage ICT in the classroom;
- cope when ICT disrupts lessons, e.g. by having fallback strategies for lessons;
- decide when to use group learning and when to use one to one learning;
- prepare for lessons;
- use the available ICT resources most effectively;
- supervise pupils when using ICT.

Strategies for involving the whole school
The integration of ICT into teaching is best achieved by involving the whole school. All the teachers should be involved in the decisions concerning its use and should plan implementations together. This approach will encourage teachers to use ICT in their teaching and will promote the adoption of innovative uses of the technology and the dissemination of good practice amongst teachers. Schools could set up self-help groups, write their own 'idiot

guides', and try out ideas on each other in a safe and friendly environment. Training can aid the integration of ICT into the whole school by helping the trainees to develop an ICT policy for their institution and by providing ideas and help for getting funding.

Self study and self help
Due to the ongoing changes in technology and the development of new forms of educational ICT, **teachers need to be equipped to learn new skills for themselves**. The teachers in our study indicated that self-teaching was a valuable form of support for helping them to use ICT. Helping teachers to help themselves can be achieved by teaching them how to use help facilities in software packages, providing them with information on sources of technical and education support on the Internet, and encouraging them to join a professional ICT in education association.

F. Expected outcomes

Clearly, the expected outcomes will depend upon the nature and content of the training and the trainees' needs. The teachers should assess their needs before embarking on the training in order to help trainers develop an appropriate programme. Expected outcomes may not only include improving ICT skills and using ICT in the curriculum, but also acquiring a more positive attitude towards using ICT in the classroom, as our research has shown that this is necessary for teachers to adopt ICT in their teaching.

The aims of a training programme should be agreed upon by the trainees and trainers before they begin. One of the most important aims of a training programme should be the effective use of ICT in the classroom in terms of the effect on pupils' learning. However, this is a long-term goal that may be difficult for trainers to achieve.

Previous research discussed earlier in the report (see section 3.4) has shown that the success of training programmes can be limited by a range of factors. For example, pressure from other demands of the curriculum can erode the time needed by teachers to prepare for ICT use in their lessons. Training courses should therefore include coping strategies to help teachers prioritise ICT use in their teaching. This research suggests that trainers need to consider other factors that might influence the outcomes of any training provided.

G. Assessment of trainees

The assessment of trainees will be dependent upon the nature and content of the training as well as the expected outcomes. Some of the NOF training providers are including skills audits or using their own, or TTA produced needs identification materials to assess teachers' training requirements. Assessment can be conducted informally during the training and also in more formal ways through the use of assignments, tests and certificates. Clearly some teachers may acquire some skills more easily than others. For example, teachers may gain new ICT skills quite rapidly but still be unwilling to change their teaching practice to use ICT in the classroom.

The types of assessment that can be used include:

- for ICT skills, the European Computer Driving Licence test, which would give the trainees a useful qualification in ICT (see www.bcs.org.uk);
- for using ICT in the classroom, certificated course assignments such as lesson plans, an evaluation of teachers' use of a software package with pupils, planning a new scheme of work to include ICT use within a subject, and devising homework for pupils requiring the use of ICT;

- keeping a record for a term of ICT use in the classroom;
- reporting on using ICT to colleagues over the Internet;
- running sessions for school colleagues on using ICT.

H. Evaluation of training

When evaluating the effects of the training and its successes, trainers need to consider what the aims were, what the attitudes of the trainees were beforehand, what opportunities the trainees had to put into practice what had been taught during the training, and what the school context is.

There are a variety of ways of measuring the success of the training: its impact on teachers' use of ICT, on improvement in practice, on teachers' abilities to help themselves, and on their sustained use of ICT in their teaching. Research has shown that teachers who have followed training courses in the past are sometimes unable to take up the use of ICT in their teaching for any length of time because too many barriers arise. Therefore, the evaluation of the training should include long-term measures to determine whether or not the trainees have continued to use ICT some time after the training has finished.

Professional Development Chart

This section presents the overview of the chart followed by more detailed charts for the three sections: inputs, processes and outputs.

Inputs

A. TRAINEE FACTORS	B. SCHOOL CONTEXT
1. Professional role 2. Level of ICT experience/knowledge	1. Level of ICT resources available 2. ICT delivery strategy 3. School management style

Processes

C. NATURE OF TRAINING	D. SUPPORTING ACTIVITIES AND MATERIALS	E. FOCUS OF TRAINING
1. Location of training 2. Training process	1. Information on software and hardware available 2. Opportunities for discussing issues with others 3. Lesson plans and schemes of work 4. Ideas and help for obtaining funding 5. Follow up activities: on-line help, handouts, professional ICT in education associations, learning communities	1. Basic ICT skills 2. Advanced ICT skills 3. Use of ICT in teaching and learning 4. Improved motivation by emphasising the advantages of using ICT 5. Improved motivation by developing strategies to overcome barriers to using ICT 6. Strategies for involving the whole school 7. Self study and self help

Outputs

F. EXPECTED OUTCOMES	G. ASSESSMENT OF TRAINEES	H. EVALUATION OF TRAINING

INPUTS

A. TRAINEE FACTORS	B. SCHOOL CONTEXT
1. Professional role a. ICT/IT co-ordinators and teachers b. senior managers c. other class teachers d. librarians e. IT support staff f. administrators g. advisors/mentors h. teacher educators **2. Level of ICT experience/knowledge** a. none b. personal use only c. occasional use in teaching d. regular use of basic forms of ICT in teaching e. extensive use of ICT for teaching and learning f. educational ICT – innovative use of ICT in teaching	**1. Level of ICT resources available** a. level of school/home provision and access b. regularity and frequency of access c. types of hardware and software d. network/Internet access or standalone **2. ICT delivery strategy** a. ICT/IT taught across the curriculum b. ICT/IT taught as a separate subject c. combination of both a and b d. using ICT within all subjects **3. School management style** a. support from senior management b. support from an ICT/IT co-ordinator c. support from a subject teacher d. all teachers responsible for ICT

PROCESSES

C. NATURE OF TRAINING	
1. Location of training	**2. Training process**
a. school	a. independent learning
b. college	b. hands on sessions
c. LEA centre	c. group discussions
d. conferences	d. lectures
e. distance learning	e. seminars
i. web site	f. mentoring
ii. closed community	g. discussion with other professionals
iii. paper materials	h. international links
iv. CD-ROMs	i. use of the Internet
v. virtual classroom	

D. SUPPORTING ACTIVITIES AND MATERIALS
1. Information on software and hardware available
2. Opportunities for discussing issues with others
3. Lesson plans and schemes of work
4. Ideas and help for obtaining funding
5. Follow up activities: on-line help, handouts, professional ICT in education associations, learning communities

E. FOCUS OF TRAINING

1. **Basic ICT skills**

2. **Advanced ICT skills**

3. **Use of ICT in teaching and learning**
   a. development of appropriate pedagogical practices
   b. fitting ICT into the subject curriculum
   c. how to combine ICT with other activities
   d. ideas for using ICT in the classroom
   e. use of subject specific software
   f. information on how ICT contributes to children's learning
   g. accommodating the different abilities of pupils and the pace at which they learn
   h. developing progression in pupils' learning
   i. how to assess pupils' ICT knowledge and skills
   j. how to assess pupils' achievements in subjects when using ICT

4. **Improved motivation by emphasising the advantages of using ICT**
   a. Advantages for pupils
      i. increased motivation
      ii. enhanced learning
      iii. increased interest, enjoyment and concentration
      iv. greater control over their learning
      v. ICT skills for their future careers
   b. advantages for teaching
      i. increased diversity in teaching activities and strategies
      ii. access to better and more diverse resources
      iii. lessons being more enjoyable, interesting, diverse and fun for the teachers
   c. advantages for teachers' personal and professional tasks
      i. greater awareness of the uses of ICT for personal and professional tasks
      ii. increased confidence in using ICT
      iii. enhanced career prospects

5. **Improved motivation by developing strategies to overcome barriers to using ICT**
   a. managing ICT in the classroom
   b. how to cope when ICT disrupts lessons
   c. when to use group/one to one learning
   d. how to prepare for lessons
   e. how to use available ICT resources most effectively
   f. supervision of pupils when using ICT

6. **Strategies for involving the whole school**
   a. fitting the use of ICT into the whole institution
   b. development of an ICT policy for the institution
   c. including all staff in decision making processes

7. **Self study and self help**

OUTPUTS

F. EXPECTED OUTCOMES
a. improved ICT skills for teachers b. ideas of how to use ICT in the classroom c. changes in classroom practice d. integration of ICT into the curriculum e. enhanced learning for pupils f. improved motivation to use ICT

G. ASSESSMENT OF TRAINEES
a. assignments, tests and certificates b. changes in the curriculum c. design and implementation of projects d. informal/formal e. within/outside of the institution

H. EVALUATION OF TRAINING
a. reports from trainees b. success indicated by assessment of trainees c. other experts within/outside of the institution

REFERENCES

ACITT (1997). *The Informatics Pack for Key Stage 3*. Barking and Dagenham LEA.

Ajzen, I. (1985). From intentions to actions: A theory of planned action. In J. Kuhl and J. Beckman (Eds.) *Action Control: From Cognition to Behavior* (pp. 11-39). New York: Springer.

Ajzen, I. (1988). *Attitudes, Personality and Behavior*. Milton Keynes: Open University Press.

Ames, C. (1992). Classroom goals, structures and student motivation. *Journal of Educational Psychology*, 84 (3), 261-71.

Andrews, P. (1995). Teachers' perceptions of the availability of computer hardware. *Journal of Computer Assisted Learning*, 11, 90-8.

Bliss, J., Chandra, P. A. J. & Cox, M. J. (1988). Introducing computers into a school - management issues. *Computers and Education*, 12(1), 57-61.

British Educational Suppliers Association (1998). *Information and Communications Technology* in *UK Schools*. London: BESA.

Brummelhuis, A. C. A. & Tuijnman, A. C. (1992). *Factors Determining the Degree of Computer Implementation: A Comparison between Six Educational Systems*. Paper presented at the European Conference on Educational Research, Enschede, The Netherlands.

Brummelhuis, A. T. & Plomp, T. J. (1994). Computers in primary and secondary education: The interest of an individual teacher or a school policy. *Computers and Education*, 22 (4), 291-9.

The Cognition and Technology Group (1997). *The Jasper Project: Lessons in Curriculum, Instruction, Assessment, and Professional Development*. London: Lawrence Erlbaum Associates.

Cox, M. J. (1994). An overview of the problems and issues associated with the uptake of computers in the United Kingdom education institutions. *Visions for Teaching and Learning, Educomp '94 Proceedings* (pp 233 – 47). Malaysian Council for Computers in Education.

Cox, M. J. (1997a). *The Effects of Information Technology on Students' Motivation. Final Report*. Coventry/London: NCET/King's College London.

Cox, M. J. (1997b). Identification of the changes in attitude and pedagogical practices needed to enable teachers to use Information Technology in the school curriculum. In D. Passey & B. Samways (Eds.) *Information Technology Supporting Change through Teacher Education*. London: Chapman Hall.

Cox, M. J. (1998). Don't throw the baby out with the bath water. *Computers Don't Bite: Teachers*. (p.16). BBC.

Cox, M. J. (1999). Motivating pupils through the use of ICT. In M. Leask, & N. Pachler (Eds.) *Learning to Teach using ICT in the Secondary School* (pp 19-35). London: Routledge.

Cox, M. J., Preston, C., & Cox, K. M. J. (1999). *What Motivates Teachers to Use ICT?* Paper presented at the British Educational Research Annual Conference, Brighton.

Cox, M. J. & Rhodes, V. J. (1990). *Current Practices and Policies for Using Computers in Primary Schools - Implications for Training.* INTER Occasional Paper 15/90. Swindon, UK: Economic and Social Research Council.

Cox, M. J, Rhodes, V. & Hall, J. (1988). The use of Computer Assisted Learning in primary schools: Some factors affecting the uptake. *Computers and Education*, 12 (1), 173-178.

Davis, F. D., Bagozzi, R. P. & Warshaw, P. R. (1989). User acceptance of computer technology: A comparison of two theoretical models. *Management Science,* 35(8), 982-1003.

Department for Education and Employment (1995). *Superhighways for Education*. London: HMSO.

Department for Education and Employment (1998a). *Survey of Information and Communications Technology in Schools*. Statistical Bulletin issue no.11/98. London: The Stationery Office.

Department for Education and Employment (1998b). *Teachers Meeting the Challenge of Change*. Green paper. London: DfEE.

Department for Education and Employment (1998c). *Teaching: High Status, High Standards*. Circular 4/98. (http://www.open.gov.uk/dfee/dfeehome.htm).

Desforges, C. (1995). How does experience affect theoretical knowledge for teaching? *Learning and Instruction*, 5, 385-400.

Eisenstadt, M. & Vincent, T. (Ed.) (1998). *The Knowledge Web: Learning and Collaborating on the Net*. London: Kogan Page.

Fishbein, M. & Ajzen, I. (1975). *Belief, Attitude, Intention and Behavior: An Introduction to Theory and Research*. Reading, MA: Addison-Wesley.

Fullan, M. (1991). *The New Meaning of Educational Change*. London: Cassell.

Gardner, D. G., Dukes, R. L. & Discenza, R. (1993). Computer use, self-confidence, and attitudes: A causal analysis. *Computers in Human Behaviour*, 9, 427-40.

Goldstein, G. (1997). *Information Technology in English Schools: A Commentary on Inspection Findings 1995-6.* Coventry: NCET/OFSTED.

Gross, R.D. (1992). *Psychology: The Science of Mind and Behaviour*. London: Hodder & Stoughton.

Harris, S. & Preston, C. (1993). *Software in Schools*. Slough: NFER/NCET.

Jones, S. (Ed.) (1997). *Virtual Culture: Identity and Communication in Cybersociety*. London: Sage.

Karahanna, E. & Straub, D. W. (1999). Information Technology adoption across time: A cross-sectional comparison of pre-adoption and post-adoption beliefs. *MIS Quarterly*, 23 (2), 183-213.

Kim, Y. (2000). *Teachers' Attitudes towards Computers: A Primary Factor Affecting Computer Uptake in the Classroom*. Doctoral Thesis. London: King's College London.

Mason R (Ed.) (1994). *Using Communications Media in Open and Flexible Learning*. London: Kogan Page.

Mason, R. (1998). *Globalising Education Trends and Applications*. London: Kogan Page.

National Council for Educational Technology (1994). *Integrated Learning Systems. A Report of the Pilot Evaluation of ILS in the UK*. Coventry: NCET.

New Opportunities Fund (1999). *Current Education Initiatives*. www.nof.org.uk.

Pelgrum, W. J. & Plomp, T. (1991). *The Use of Computers in Education Worldwide: Results from the IEA 'Computers in Education' Survey in 19 Education Systems*. Oxford: Pergamon Press.

Phillips, R., Bailey, M., Fisher, T. & Harrison, C. (1999). Questioning teachers about their use of portable computers. *Journal of Computer Assisted Learning*, 12 (2), 149-161.

Preston, C. (1999). Building on-line professional development communities for schools, professional associations or LEAs. In M. Leask & N. Pachler (Eds.) *Learning to Teach Using ICT in the Secondary School* (pp 210 – 225). London: Routledge.

Preston, C. (2000). Industry and Education Partnership. In M. Leask (Ed.) *ICT Issues in Schools*. London: Routledge (in press).

Preston, C., Mannova, B. & Lengel, L. (2000). Collaboration through Technology Now and in the Future: Linking New Europe with the World. In L. Lengel (Ed.), *Culture and Technology in the New Europe: Civic Discourse in Post Communist Nations*. New York: Ablex (in press).

Qualifications and Curriculum Authority (2000). www.qca.org.uk.

Rheingold, H. (1991). *Virtual Reality*. New York, NY: Simon & Schuster.

Ridgway, J. & Passey, D. (1991). *Effective In-service Education for Teachers in Information Technology*. Coventry: NCET.

Selwyn, N. (1997). Teaching Information Technology to the 'computer shy': A theoretical perspective on a practical problem. *Journal of Vocational Education and Training*, 10(3), 395-408.

Sinko, M. & Lehtinen, E. (1999). The challenges of ICT in Finnish education. *Atena Kustannus*. Finland: Jyväskylä.

Somekh, B. (1989). Action research and collaborative school development. In R. McBride (Ed.), *The In-service Training of Teachers: Some Issues and Perspectives.* Brighton: Falmer Press.

Somekh, B. & Davis, N. (Eds.) (1997). *Using Information Technology Effectively in Teaching and Learning.* London: Routledge.

Squires, D. & McDougall, A. (1994). *Choosing and Using Educational Software: A Teacher's Guide.* London: Falmer Press.

Stradling, B., Sims, D. & Jamison, J. (1994). *Portable Computers Pilot Evaluation Report.* Coventry: NCET.

Tabachnick, B. G. & Fidell, L. S. (1996). *Using Multivariate Statistics* (3rd Ed.). New York: Harper Collins.

Teacher Training Agency (1999). ICT Identification of Your Training Needs Primary and Secondary CD-ROMs. (To order, tel: 0845-606-0323).

Underwood, J. (1997). Breaking the cycle of ignorance: Information Technology and the professional development of teachers. In D. Passey & B. Samways (Eds.) *Information Technology Supporting Change through Teacher Education* (pp 155 – 160). London: Chapman Hall.

Watson, D. M. (Ed.) (1993). *IMPACT - An Evaluation of the IMPACT of the Information Technology on Children's Achievements in Primary and Secondary Schools.* London: King's College London.

Weiner, B. (1990). The history of motivational research. *Journal of Educational Psychology*, 82 (4), 616-627.

USEFUL CONTACTS AND WEB SITES

Organisations who participated in the study

MirandaNet
The Institute of Education,
University of London
20 Bedford Way
WC1H OAL
enquiries@mirandanet.ac.uk
www.mirandanet.ac.uk

National Association of Co-ordinators and Teachers of IT (ACITT)
IAS,
The Westbury Centre,
Ripple Road,
Barking,
Essex, IG11 7PT
www.acitt.org.uk

TeacherNetUK
De Montfort University
Polhill Avenue
Bedford, Bedfordshire,
Tnetuk@dmu.ac.uk
www.teachernetuk.org.uk

Other web sites named in the report

BBC
www.bbc.co.uk/education/home/

British Computer Society (BCS)
www.bcs.org.uk

British Educational and Communications Technology Agency (BECTa)
www.becta.org.uk

British Educational Suppliers Association (BESA)
www.besanet.org.uk

Compaq Computers Ltd.
www.compaq.co.uk/education

Department for Education and Employment (DfEE)
www.dfee.gov.uk

ICL
www.icl.com/government/education.htm

IT in Teacher Education (ITTE)
http://itte.ntu.ac.uk

The IT Network
www.itnetwork.org.uk

Micros and Primary Education (MAPE)
www.mape.org.uk

Microsoft Corporation
www.microsoft.com/uk/education/

National Association of Advisors for Computers in Education (NAACE)
www.naace.org

National Grid for Learning (NGfL)
www.ngfl.gov.uk

New Opportunities Fund (NOF)
www.nof.org.uk

Oracle Ltd.
Use the link on www.mirandanet.ac.uk for information about the new www.think.com site

Qualifications and Curriculum Authority (QCA)
www.qca.org.uk

Research Machines
www.eduweb.co.uk

Teacher Training Agency (TTA)
www.teach-tta.gov.uk

Tesco Ltd.
www.schoolnet2000.com

Times Educational Supplement (TES)
www.tes.co.uk/online

Times Higher Education Supplement (THES)
www.thes.co.uk

Virtual Teachers' Centre
www.vtc.ngfl.gov.uk

APPENDIX A - Correlations between perceived ease of use and usefulness factors and frequency of ICT use in teaching

			QUESTIONNAIRE ITEM	1	2	3	4	5	6	7	8	9
PERCEIVED EASE OF USE		1	I find it easy to think of ways to use IT in teaching	1.00	-0.43	-0.07	-0.16	-0.17	-0.05	0.11	-0.15	-0.15
		2	I often have difficulties using software/hardware	-0.43	1.00	-0.01	0.17	0.06	0.21	-0.10	-0.09	0.10
		3	using IT makes preparing for lessons more time-consuming	-0.07	-0.01	1.00	0.59	0.22	0.27	-0.22	-0.02	-0.01
		4	using IT makes preparing for lessons more difficult	-0.16	0.17	0.59	1.00	0.27	0.20	-0.13	0.06	-0.04
		5	using IT makes it more difficult to control the class	-0.17	0.06	0.22	0.27	1.00	0.26	-0.33	-0.01	-0.22
		6	hardware/software problems often disrupt my lessons	-0.05	0.21	0.27	0.20	0.26	1.00	-0.23	0.06	0.27
		7	I am satisfied with the IT resources available to me	0.11	-0.10	-0.22	-0.13	-0.33	-0.23	1.00	0.05	-0.13
		8	I don't have enough time to use IT	-0.15	-0.09	-0.02	0.06	-0.01	0.06	0.05	1.00	0.36
		9	I would like more technical support	-0.15	0.10	-0.01	-0.04	-0.22	0.27	-0.13	0.36	1.00
		10	I want more staff support	-0.18	0.17	0.26	0.25	0.03	0.13	-0.16	0.37	0.49
		11	using IT in teaching is counter-productive due to insufficient resources	-0.38	0.27	0.33	0.05	0.14	0.51	-0.43	0.17	0.16
		12	I want to use educational software more in my teaching	0.17	0.11	0.03	-0.01	-0.07	0.26	-0.37	-0.09	0.22
PERCEIVED USEFULNESS	Teaching	13	using IT makes lessons more interesting for me	0.51	-0.27	-0.15	-0.21	-0.34	0.02	0.03	-0.04	0.18
		14	using IT makes lessons more difficult for me	-0.59	0.42	0.30	0.42	0.36	0.15	-0.22	-0.04	-0.11
		15	using IT makes lessons less fun for me	-0.37	0.18	-0.06	0.12	0.29	-0.11	0.02	0.02	-0.18
		16	using IT makes my lessons more diverse	0.24	-0.06	-0.10	-0.21	-0.12	-0.10	0.03	0.08	0.05
		17	using IT has improved my presentation of materials	0.22	-0.10	-0.13	-0.26	-0.20	-0.13	0.01	-0.04	0.11
		18	using IT in my teaching is not enjoyable	-0.33	0.22	0.09	0.15	0.05	0.19	-0.09	0.13	-0.04
		19	using IT restricts the content of my lessons	-0.14	0.04	0.21	0.36	0.29	0.05	0.00	0.14	-0.14
	Pupils	20	using IT reduces pupils' motivation	-0.43	0.28	0.12	0.24	0.32	0.05	-0.12	0.00	-0.13
		21	using IT impairs pupils' learning	-0.14	0.16	0.09	0.21	0.18	0.15	-0.04	0.22	-0.14
		22	using IT makes lessons more fun for pupils	0.05	-0.05	-0.13	-0.36	-0.09	-0.04	-0.05	-0.14	0.15
	Personal/Prof. Dev.	23	using IT in my teaching has given me greater access for personal IT use	0.02	-0.13	-0.21	-0.37	-0.26	-0.07	0.27	0.23	0.31
		24	using IT in my teaching gives me more power in the school	0.05	-0.08	-0.08	-0.09	-0.10	-0.07	0.18	0.09	0.06
		25	using IT in my teaching gives me more prestige	0.05	-0.12	-0.10	-0.14	-0.14	-0.07	0.16	0.00	0.07
		26	using IT in my teaching enhances my career prospects	0.12	-0.13	-0.22	-0.26	-0.16	-0.07	0.13	-0.09	-0.04
		27	using IT in my teaching has given me more confidence using computers	0.17	-0.22	-0.03	-0.16	-0.04	-0.03	0.18	0.05	0.21
		28	using IT in teaching has given me greater awareness of its uses	0.10	-0.15	-0.17	-0.25	-0.02	-0.02	0.10	0.04	0.31
		29	using IT makes my administration more efficient	0.10	-0.11	-0.20	-0.32	-0.21	-0.27	0.24	0.02	-0.09
FREQUENCY OF ICT USE IN TEACHING				0.49	-0.31	0.08	-0.06	-0.14	-0.21	0.46	-0.07	-0.08

			10	11	12	13	14	15	16	17	18	19	20	21	22	23	24	25	26	27	28	29
PERCEIVED EASE OF USE		1	-0.18	-0.38	0.17	0.51	-0.59	-0.37	0.24	0.22	-0.33	-0.14	-0.43	-0.14	0.05	0.02	0.05	0.05	0.12	0.17	0.10	0.10
		2	0.17	0.27	0.11	-0.27	0.42	0.18	-0.06	-0.10	0.22	0.04	0.28	0.16	-0.05	-0.13	-0.08	-0.12	-0.13	-0.22	-0.15	-0.11
		3	0.26	0.33	0.03	-0.15	0.30	-0.06	-0.10	-0.13	0.09	0.21	0.12	0.09	-0.13	-0.21	-0.08	-0.10	-0.22	-0.03	-0.17	-0.20
		4	0.25	0.05	-0.01	-0.21	0.42	0.12	-0.21	-0.26	0.15	0.36	0.24	0.21	-0.36	-0.37	-0.09	-0.14	-0.26	-0.16	-0.25	-0.32
		5	0.03	0.14	-0.07	-0.34	0.36	0.29	-0.12	-0.20	0.05	0.29	0.32	0.18	-0.09	-0.26	-0.10	-0.14	-0.16	-0.04	-0.02	-0.21
		6	0.13	0.51	0.26	0.02	0.15	-0.11	-0.10	-0.13	0.19	0.05	0.05	0.15	-0.04	-0.07	-0.07	-0.07	-0.07	-0.03	-0.02	-0.27
		7	-0.16	-0.43	-0.37	0.03	-0.22	0.02	0.03	0.01	-0.09	0.00	-0.12	-0.04	-0.05	0.27	0.18	0.16	0.13	0.18	0.10	0.24
		8	0.37	0.17	-0.09	-0.04	-0.04	0.02	0.08	-0.04	0.13	0.14	0.00	0.22	-0.14	0.23	0.09	0.00	-0.09	0.05	0.04	0.02
		9	0.49	0.16	0.22	0.18	-0.11	-0.18	0.05	0.11	-0.04	-0.14	-0.13	-0.14	0.15	0.31	0.06	0.07	-0.04	0.21	0.31	-0.09
		10	1.00	0.26	0.13	0.00	0.08	-0.01	0.12	-0.07	-0.09	0.00	0.00	-0.10	0.02	0.16	0.06	-0.08	-0.14	0.28	0.28	-0.16
		11	0.26	1.00	0.15	-0.26	0.26	-0.03	0.05	-0.06	0.24	0.04	0.02	0.15	0.03	-0.02	-0.01	-0.07	-0.02	-0.11	-0.05	-0.04
		12	0.13	0.15	1.00	0.34	-0.01	-0.19	0.30	-0.01	0.08	-0.09	-0.29	0.03	0.10	-0.02	0.10	0.04	0.05	0.06	0.16	-0.03
PERCEIVED USEFULNESS	Teaching	13	0.00	-0.26	0.34	1.00	-0.55	-0.60	0.33	0.21	-0.23	-0.36	-0.46	-0.37	0.07	0.35	0.10	0.13	0.15	0.34	0.33	-0.09
		14	0.08	0.26	-0.01	-0.55	1.00	0.41	-0.28	-0.32	0.22	0.34	0.37	0.26	-0.21	-0.21	-0.02	-0.03	-0.10	-0.29	-0.28	-0.11
		15	-0.01	-0.03	-0.19	-0.60	0.41	1.00	-0.30	-0.22	0.08	0.36	0.44	0.28	-0.25	-0.23	-0.01	-0.02	-0.09	-0.19	-0.20	0.08
		16	0.12	0.05	0.30	0.33	-0.28	-0.30	1.00	0.21	-0.10	-0.33	-0.52	-0.17	0.16	0.17	0.32	0.21	0.19	0.44	0.53	0.24
		17	-0.07	-0.06	-0.01	0.21	-0.32	-0.22	0.21	1.00	-0.31	-0.39	-0.28	-0.39	0.40	0.33	0.22	0.19	0.18	0.23	0.18	0.33
		18	-0.09	0.24	0.08	-0.23	0.22	0.08	-0.10	-0.31	1.00	0.33	0.31	0.61	-0.23	-0.27	-0.37	-0.28	-0.35	-0.25	-0.23	-0.09
		19	0.00	0.04	-0.09	-0.36	0.34	0.36	-0.33	-0.39	0.33	1.00	0.33	0.65	-0.40	-0.37	-0.14	-0.16	-0.24	-0.41	-0.48	-0.10
	Pupils	20	0.00	0.02	-0.29	-0.46	0.37	0.44	-0.52	-0.28	0.31	0.33	1.00	0.37	-0.31	-0.19	-0.22	-0.28	-0.23	-0.37	-0.39	-0.14
		21	-0.10	0.15	0.03	-0.37	0.26	0.28	-0.17	-0.39	0.61	0.65	0.37	1.00	-0.41	-0.29	-0.12	-0.20	-0.35	-0.36	-0.35	-0.13
		22	0.02	0.03	0.10	0.07	-0.21	-0.25	0.16	0.40	-0.23	-0.40	-0.31	-0.41	1.00	0.17	0.21	0.26	0.17	0.25	0.26	0.08
	Personal/Prof. Dev.	23	0.16	-0.02	-0.02	0.35	-0.21	-0.23	0.17	0.33	-0.27	-0.37	-0.19	-0.29	0.17	1.00	0.31	0.30	0.39	0.52	0.53	0.19
		24	0.06	-0.01	0.10	0.10	-0.02	-0.01	0.32	0.22	-0.37	-0.14	-0.22	-0.12	0.21	0.31	1.00	0.78	0.44	0.29	0.29	0.14
		25	-0.08	-0.07	0.04	0.13	-0.03	-0.02	0.21	0.19	-0.28	-0.16	-0.28	-0.20	0.26	0.30	0.78	1.00	0.52	0.26	0.20	0.03
		26	-0.14	-0.02	0.05	0.15	-0.10	-0.09	0.19	0.18	-0.35	-0.24	-0.23	-0.35	0.17	0.39	0.44	0.52	1.00	0.34	0.28	0.15
		27	0.28	-0.11	0.06	0.34	-0.29	-0.19	0.44	0.23	-0.25	-0.41	-0.37	-0.36	0.25	0.52	0.29	0.26	0.34	1.00	0.86	0.14
		28	0.28	-0.05	0.16	0.33	-0.28	-0.20	0.53	0.18	-0.23	-0.48	-0.39	-0.35	0.26	0.53	0.29	0.20	0.28	0.86	1.00	0.10
		29	-0.16	-0.04	-0.03	-0.09	-0.11	0.08	0.24	0.33	-0.09	-0.10	-0.14	-0.13	0.08	0.19	0.14	0.03	0.15	0.14	0.10	1.00
ICT USE			-0.07	-0.46	-0.38	0.35	-0.38	-0.28	-0.01	0.22	-0.39	-0.13	-0.22	-0.27	0.12	0.14	0.14	0.11	-0.01	0.18	0.04	0.01

APPENDIX B – ICT IN EDUCATION QUESTIONNAIRE

For the purpose of this questionnaire we have used the term ICT (Information and Communications Technologies) which refers to the use of the Internet, E-mail, video conferencing and other forms of communication technologies in addition to more traditional information technologies.

The information from this questionnaire will be used to develop a guide to effective ICT professional development programmes for staff in schools. The respondents will be cited in the acknowledgements but no names or institutions will be linked to particular comments in any publications and consequently no institution will be identifiable. However, we would be grateful if respondents would give their names so that, if possible, they can be contacted for an interview concerning particular aspects of the questionnaire.

All respondents are invited to a focus meeting on the 29th January 1999 where you will have the opportunity to ask questions about the staff training in your school. You will also receive a copy of the practical guide and resources pack. Further details will be sent nearer the time.

1. Personal Information

1.1. Name: ______________________

1.2. Age: __________ **1.3. Sex:** **M / F**

1.4. Contact address: ______________________

____

1.5. Contact telephone number: ______________________

1.6. Contact fax number: ______________________

1.7. E-mail address: ______________________

1.8. Name of institution: ______________________

1.9. Job title: ______________________

1.10. What are your current teaching commitments? ______________________

____

1.11. Are you obliged to teach IT? **yes / no**

1.12. If yes, who or what requires you to teach IT (e.g. head teacher, national curriculum, etc.)

____

1.13. What are your senior management responsibilities (e.g. staff training, curriculum delivery)?

____

____

1.14. Main teaching subjects and length of time spent teaching (if appropriate):

Please indicate the main subjects you have taught throughout your career and the length of time you have spent teaching them:

Subject taught	No. of years taught

1.15. What subject(s) were you initially trained to teach (e.g. Mathematics):

____

1.16. Which phase do you teach in (e.g. primary)? ____________________

2. Personal use of computers

If you do not have access to a computer for personal use at home please move on to section 3.

2.1. Who owns the computer you use outside of school (e.g. you, your husband/wife/partner)?

____

2.2. How many people share access to this computer? ____________________

2.3. Please indicate which type of computer you use:

Desktop PC		Palmtop	
Desktop Apple Mac		Game console	
Laptop		E-mate	
Other (please specify)			

2.4. Please indicate which of the following tasks you perform on this computer:

Loading software	
Formatting disks	
Virus checking	
File management	
Connecting it to external devices	
Using help-facilities	
Creating sub-directories	

2.5. – 2.13. Use of different forms of ICT

Please indicate the approximate year when you first and last used each of the following forms of ICT outside of your workplace (if appropriate).

Please also indicate the three forms of ICT you use most frequently outside of your workplace by writing 1, 2 and 3 for the form you use with the first, second and third highest frequency respectively.

		Year first used	Year last used	Don't use	Most frequent use (please write 1, 2, & 3)
2.5.	Word processing				
2.6.	Spreadsheets				
2.7.	Databases				
2.8.	Desk-top publishing				
2.9.	Art/graphics software				
2.10.	CD-ROM software				
2.11.	E-mail				
2.12.	World Wide Web				
2.13.	Games				
2.14.	Other *(please specify)*				

2.15. – 2.16. Please fill in the following information about your personal computer and use if you know it:

2.15. Total RAM	
2.16. Total ROM	

2.17. Do you have access to the Internet at home? **yes / no**

If no please move on to section 3.

2.18. Which Internet service providers and software do you use to access the Internet outside of your workplace?

INTERNET SERVICE PROVIDERS		SOFTWARE	
RM Internet for learning		**Telnet**	
Pipex		**Eudora**	
Demon		**Simeon**	
AOL		**Netscape**	
Janet		**Office**	
Super Janet		**Outlook**	
ONYX		**Internet Explorer**	
Compuserve		**Other *(please specify)***	
Other *(please specify)*			

2.19. – 2.23. Please fill in the following information about your personal computer and use if you know it:

2.19. Make of modem		
2.20. Modem speed		
2.21. Personal or shared E-mail address?	**personal / shared**	
2.22. Average hours per week spent on-line for personal use		
2.23. Average number of personal messages you send (S) and receive (R) each week	**S =**	**R =**

2.24. Please indicate which web-sites you have accessed most frequently for your personal use:

____

____

____

3. Use of computers in school or other educational establishment

For sections 3, 4 and 5 teaching refers to 'face to face' contact with pupils and does not include preparation and other such tasks.

3.1. – 3.11. Use of different forms of ICT in your teaching/education work

Please indicate the approximate year when you first and last used (if appropriate) each of the following forms of ICT in your teaching/education work:

		Year first used	Year last used	Don' t use
3.1.	Word processing			
3.2.	Spreadsheets			
3.3.	Databases			
3.4.	Desk-top publishing			
3.5.	Art/graphics software			
3.6.	Modelling			
3.7.	Measurement and control			
3.8.	Subject specific software			
3.9.	CD-ROM			
3.10.	E-mail			
3.11.	World Wide Web			
3.12.	Other *(please specify)*			

3.13. – 3.23. Please indicate how often you use ICT in your teaching/education work.

Please answer each of the following questions by circling the appropriate response.

		never	about an hour each month	about an hour each week	several hours a week	more than an hour a day
3.13.	Word processing	1	2	3	4	5
3.14.	Spreadsheets	1	2	3	4	5
3.15.	Databases	1	2	3	4	5
3.16.	Desk-top publishing	1	2	3	4	5
3.17.	Art/graphics software	1	2	3	4	5
3.18.	Modelling	1	2	3	4	5
3.19.	Measurement and control	1	2	3	4	5
3.20.	Subject specific software	1	2	3	4	5
3.21.	CD-ROM	1	2	3	4	5
3.22.	E-mail	1	2	3	4	5
3.23.	World Wide Web	1	2	3	4	5

3.24. **Please indicate which of the following web-sites you have explored (E) and which of these you value highly (V).**

	E	V		E	V
Tesco SchoolNet			TeacherNet UK		
RM			Miranda Net		
Campus 2000			Times Education Supplement		
Teacher Training Agency			BBC		
The Virtual Teachers' Centre			Microsoft		
ICL			Other		
Times Higher Education Supplement					

4. Using IT in your teaching

If your work does not involve teaching then please move to section 6.

This section addresses your use of information technology in your teaching, both as a separate subject and in other curriculum areas, and should be completed by IT teachers and other subject teachers. Section 5 will address your use of communication technologies, such as the Internet and E-mail, in your teaching.

4.1. – 4.7. Integrating IT into your teaching

Please answer each of the following questions by circling the appropriate response.

		strongly disagree	disagree	neutral	agree	Strongly agree
4.1.	I find it easy to think of ways to use IT in my teaching	1	2	3	4	5
4.2.	I would like to use more educational software in my teaching	1	2	3	4	5
4.3.	I often have difficulties using software/ hardware	1	2	3	4	5
4.4.	I am satisfied with the level of IT resources available to me	1	2	3	4	5
4.5.	I don't have enough time to use IT as much as I would like	1	2	3	4	5
4.6.	I would like to receive more technical support	1	2	3	4	5
4.7.	I would like to receive more support from the other members of staff for using IT	1	2	3	4	5

4.8. – 4.27. The advantages and disadvantages of using IT in your teaching. Please answer each of the following questions by circling the appropriate response.

Using IT in my teaching:

		strongly disagree	disagree	neutral	agree	strongly agree
4.8.	makes my lessons more interesting for me	1	2	3	4	5
4.9.	makes my lessons more difficult for me	1	2	3	4	5
4.10.	makes my lessons less fun for me	1	2	3	4	5
4.11.	makes my lessons more diverse	1	2	3	4	5
4.12.	reduces pupils motivation	1	2	3	4	5
4.13.	has improved the presentation of material in my lessons	1	2	3	4	5
4.14.	impairs pupils' learning	1	2	3	4	5

4.15.	**has allowed me greater access to a computer for my personal and professional use**	**1**	**2**	**3**	**4**	**5**
4.16.	**is not enjoyable**	**1**	**2**	**3**	**4**	**5**
4.17.	**gives me more power in the school**	**1**	**2**	**3**	**4**	**5**
4.18.	**gives me more prestige**	**1**	**2**	**3**	**4**	**5**
4.19.	**makes preparing for lessons more time-consuming**	**1**	**2**	**3**	**4**	**5**
4.20.	**gives me access to better funding**	**1**	**2**	**3**	**4**	**5**
4.21.	**restricts the content of my lessons**	**1**	**2**	**3**	**4**	**5**
4.22.	**makes my administration more efficient**	**1**	**2**	**3**	**4**	**5**
4.23.	**enhances my career prospects**	**1**	**2**	**3**	**4**	**5**
4.24.	**makes preparing for lessons more difficult**	**1**	**2**	**3**	**4**	**5**
4.25.	**makes the lessons more fun for the pupils**	**1**	**2**	**3**	**4**	**5**
4.26.	**makes it more difficult to control the class**	**1**	**2**	**3**	**4**	**5**
4.27.	**has often disrupted my lessons due to problems with hardware/software**	**1**	**2**	**3**	**4**	**5**
4.28.	**has given me more confidence in using computers**	**1**	**2**	**3**	**4**	**5**
4.29.	**has given me greater awareness of its uses**	**1**	**2**	**3**	**4**	**5**
4.30.	**can be counter-productive due to insufficient technical resources**	**1**	**2**	**3**	**4**	**5**
4.31.	**is often highly expensive**	**1**	**2**	**3**	**4**	**5**

4.32. **What do you feel are the main advantages of using IT in your teaching?**

____

____

4.33. **What do you feel are the main disadvantages of using IT in your teaching?**

____

____

5. Using the Internet in your teaching

5.1. **Where do you access the Internet?**

At home	
In the classroom	
In the staff room	
At your work desk	
In the Library	
Other ***(please specify)***	

5.2. – 5.5. Please estimate the percentage of staff and pupils in your institution with Internet addresses at home and school/college:

		0 – 25%	26 – 50%	51 – 75%	76 – 100%	Don't know
5.2.	staff with an Internet addresses in school/college					
5.3.	staff with an Internet addresses at home					
5.4.	pupils with an Internet addresses in school/college					
5.5.	pupils with an Internet addresses at home					

5.6. **In my professional role, the most useful Internet sites are:** ____________________

____

5.7. **Which on-line discussion groups and List-servs do you belong to / have belonged to in the past:**

____

5.8. **Which Internet services does your institution subscribe to for staff and pupils' use?**

____

5.9. **Have you used video conferencing?** **yes / no**

5.10. **If yes, which software package did you use and what was the educational purpose?**

Software package: ______________________________

Educational purpose: ______________________________

____

5.11. **Would you be willing to spend about 15 hours a month tutoring colleagues outside your own institution through on-line communication, if you had the right training?** **yes / no / uncertain**

5.12. **Would you like to be a member of a teachers' on-line support network?** **yes / no / uncertain**

5.13. **Is your institution developing / has developed an Intranet for staff and pupils to use?** **yes / no / uncertain**

5.14. – 5.21. National Grid for Learning (NGfL)

The DfEE has declared that every school pupil and teacher will be on-line by the year 2002 through the National Grid for Learning programme. Please answer the following questions about the NGfL by circling the appropriate response.

		strongly disagree	disagree	neutral	agree	strongly agree
5.14.	My institution is planning to make substantial use of the NGfL	1	2	3	4	5
5.15.	My institution has enough resources to take advantage of NGfL opportunities	1	2	3	4	5
5.16.	Our LEA has given us sufficient advice on the NGfL	1	2	3	4	5
5.17.	I am well informed about the NGfL	1	2	3	4	5
5.18.	I am integrating the NGfL into my teaching	1	2	3	4	5
5.19.	If every pupil had an E-mail address it would help them to learn about ICT	1	2	3	4	5
5.20.	It would be beneficial to the teaching profession if every teacher had an E-mail address	1	2	3	4	5
5.21.	I will be active in a teachers' on-line support network if I have sufficient resources	1	2	3	4	5

5.22. – 5.32. Please indicate the extent to which the following sources of information have been useful in terms of providing information on the NGfL:

		Of no use				Very useful
5.22.	Government reports	1	2	3	4	5
5.23.	Teacher Training Agency	1	2	3	4	5
5.24.	National newspapers	1	2	3	4	5
5.25.	Education press	1	2	3	4	5
5.26.	Educational computer press	1	2	3	4	5
5.27.	BECTa	1	2	3	4	5
5.28.	Colleagues	1	2	3	4	5
5.29.	Own on-line investigation	1	2	3	4	5
5.30.	Membership of a professional organisation	1	2	3	4	5
5.31.	My LEA	1	2	3	4	5
5.32.	Courses attended	1	2	3	4	5
5.33.	Conferences	1	2	3	4	5

5.34. **Please give details of any other sources of information which have been useful in terms of providing information on the NGfL?** ______________________________

____

5.35. Please indicate when you think pupils should be given free E-mail addresses:

Before teachers	
After teachers	
At the same time	
Not at all	

Why? ______________________________

____

____

5.36. – 5.47. Please indicate the extent to which you value the following aspects of using the Internet.

		Low value				High value
5.36.	Sharing my worksheets and resources	1	2	3	4	5
5.37.	Publishing my materials without payment for peers	1	2	3	4	5
5.38.	Publishing my material for unrestricted use	1	2	3	4	5
5.39.	Communication with a wider audience	1	2	3	4	5
5.40.	Discussing teaching ideas	1	2	3	4	5
5.41.	Debating learning issues	1	2	3	4	5
5.42.	Accessing professional resources	1	2	3	4	5
5.43.	Getting advice from experts	1	2	3	4	5
5.44.	Questioning peers on published class-work	1	2	3	4	5
5.45.	Following accredited courses	1	2	3	4	5
5.46.	Finding employment	1	2	3	4	5
5.47.	Increasing my professional knowledge and skills	1	2	3	4	5

5.48. What other aspects of using the Internet do you value? ______________________________

____

____

____

6. Professional development

For the following questions, in-service training refers to all forms of courses and conferences including on-line support networks and statutory school training days.

6.1. Please indicate the number of each form of in-service training in ICT education you have received:

Location	Number of courses received				
	Initial awareness course	Short special course (e.g. using databases)	Advanced course	Working conference	Longer award bearing course
In school					
In college					
LEA centre					
On-line					
Residential					

6.2. Please indicate any other support you receive for using ICT, by ticking one or more of the following:

Other member of staff	
IT co-ordinator	
Professional mentor	
Governor	
Pupil's parent	
LEA advisor	
Membership of ACITT	
Membership of MirandaNet	
Membership of TeacherNet UK	
Self-teaching	
Other (please specify)	

6.3. – 6.10. The benefits of in-service training

Please answer the following questions by circling the appropriate response.

The in-service training I have received:

		Strongly disagree	disagree	neutral	agree	strongly agree
6.3.	enhanced my ICT skills	1	2	3	4	5
6.4.	enhanced my knowledge of good practice for using ICT in my teaching	1	2	3	4	5
6.5.	allowed me to have useful discussions with other professionals	1	2	3	4	5
6.6.	gave me greater awareness of teaching materials	1	2	3	4	5
6.7.	gave me more ideas for using ICT in the classroom	1	2	3	4	5
6.8.	helped me to understand the role of the World Wide Web	1	2	3	4	5
6.9.	helped me to change my classroom practice	1	2	3	4	5
6.10.	helped me to improve staff training programmes	1	2	3	4	5

6.11. – 6.19. Please indicate the extent to which you value different forms of training:

		Low value				High value
6.11.	Basic ICT skills	1	2	3	4	5
6.12.	Advanced ICT skills	1	2	3	4	5
6.13.	Ideas for using ICT in the classroom	1	2	3	4	5
6.14.	Information on how ICT contributes to children's learning	1	2	3	4	5
6.15.	Discussions with other professionals	1	2	3	4	5
6.16.	International links	1	2	3	4	5
6.17.	Developing an ICT policy	1	2	3	4	5
6.18.	More information on the National Grid for Learning	1	2	3	4	5
6.19.	Managing ICT in the classroom	1	2	3	4	5
6.20.	Using ICT for administration	1	2	3	4	5
6.21.	Using ICT for professional development	1	2	3	4	5

6.22. Please indicate the form you would like this training to be:

Location	Number of courses received				
	Initial awareness course	Short special course (e.g. using databases)	Advanced course	Longer award bearing course	Working conference
In school					
In college					
LEA centre					
On-line					
Residential					
Other (please specify)					

6.23. Please indicate what other support would enable you to use ICT more in your teaching:

Better resources	
Funding to attend courses and conferences	
More support from other members of staff	
More support from your LEA	
On-line contact with peers and experts	
More support from ACITT	
More support from MirandaNet	
An IT co-ordinator	
Other (please specify)	

6.24. Please indicate the number of each form of in-service training in ICT education you have delivered:

Location	Number of courses received				
	Initial awareness course	Short special course (e.g. using databases)	Advanced course	Longer award bearing course	Working conference
In school					
In college					
LEA centre					
On-line					
Residential					
Other (please specify)					

6.25. How successful do you think your training contributions are *(please circle one)*?	Very un-successful	Fairly un-successful	neutral	Fairly successful	Very successful

7. Using ICT for administration

7.1. – 7.9. Please indicate who performs each of the following tasks in your institution.

	You	Clerical personnel	Other teachers	Head teacher	Other *(please specify)*
7.1. Correspondence					
7.2. Time-tabling					
7.3. Worksheets					
7.4. SEN records					
7.5. Assessment					
7.6. Pupils records (e.g. profiles, reports)					
7.7. Ordering supplies					
7.8. Budgeting					
7.9. Other school management *(please specify*					

Thank you for your time and help with our research.

FOR MIRANDANET FELLOWS AND SCHOLARS

Confidential to non-MirandaNet researcher

1. MirandaNet information

1.1. **How did you hear about MirandaNet?** ______________________

1.2. **How did you join up?** ______________________

1.3. **How long have you been a member of MirandaNet?** ______________________

1.4. **How many meetings have you attended?** ______________________

		never	every few months	once each month	once each week	several times a week
1.5.	How often do you communicate with other MirandaNet members? *(please circle one)*	1	2	3	4	5

1.6. - 1.12. The benefits of membership of MirandaNet:

Please answer each of the following questions by circling the appropriate response.

MirandaNet has enabled me to:

		strongly disagree	disagree	neutral	agree	strongly agree
1.6.	have greater awareness of the uses of ICT	1	2	3	4	5
1.7.	gain new ICT skills	1	2	3	4	5
1.8.	have the opportunity to meet like-minded individuals	1	2	3	4	5
1.9.	have specialist help and guidance	1	2	3	4	5
1.10.	keep up with advances in ICT	1	2	3	4	5
1.11.	improve my teaching	1	2	3	4	5
1.12.	improve my personal use of computers	1	2	3	4	5

1.13. **Please describe any other advantages you have experienced as a result of your membership of MirandaNet:** ______________________

____

____

____

1.14 – 1.29. Please indicate the extent to which you value the various services and opportunities offered by MirandaNet:

		Low value				High value	Don't know
1.14.	Conferences	1	2	3	4	5	
1.15.	Seminars	1	2	3	4	5	
1.16.	New hardware	1	2	3	4	5	
1.17.	New software	1	2	3	4	5	
1.18.	Product trials	1	2	3	4	5	
1.19.	Use of Internet / E-mail	1	2	3	4	5	
1.20.	Additional funding	1	2	3	4	5	
1.21.	Scholarships	1	2	3	4	5	
1.22.	Specialist help	1	2	3	4	5	
1.23.	Mentoring of scholars by fellows	1	2	3	4	5	
1.24.	Consultations for industry	1	2	3	4	5	
1.25.	Interaction with other professionals	1	2	3	4	5	
1.26.	International exchange	1	2	3	4	5	
1.27.	Audience to which I can voice my opinions	1	2	3	4	5	
1.28.	Increased ICT skills	1	2	3	4	5	
1.29.	Ideas and help for funding for ICT projects	1	2	3	4	5	

1.30. Please indicate which of the following you consider to have limited the usefulness of the help you have received:

Time	
Resources	
Poor software	
Poor hardware	
The support cover requirement	
Travelling costs	
Other (please specify)	

1.31. What other services/support would you like to receive from MirandaNet?

____

____

1.32. Please indicate for how long you wish to remain an active member of MirandaNet:

Less than a year	
1-2 years	
2-5 years	
5-10 years	
More than 10 years	

1.33. Would you continue your membership of MirandaNet if you had to pay a subscription fee? **yes / no**

1.34. **If yes, how much would you be willing to pay per year?**

£10 - £19	
£20 - £29	
£30 - £39	
£40 - £49	
£50 - £59	
£60 - £69	
More than £70	

Thank you for your time and help with our research.

FOR ACITT MEMBERS

1. ACITT information

1.1. **How did you hear about ACITT?** ______________________________

1.2. **How did you join up?** ______________________________

1.3. **How long have you been a member of ACITT?** ______________________________

1.4. **How many conferences have you attended?** ______________________________

		never	every few months	once each month	once each week	several times a week
1.5.	How often do you communicate with other ACITT members? *(please circle one)*	1	2	3	4	5

1.6. - 1.12. The benefits of membership of ACITT:

Please answer each of the following questions by circling the appropriate response.

ACITT has enabled me to:

		strongly disagree	disagree	neutral	agree	strongly agree
1.6.	have greater awareness of the uses of IT	1	2	3	4	5
1.7.	gain new IT skills	1	2	3	4	5
1.8.	have the opportunity to meet like-minded individuals	1	2	3	4	5
1.9.	have specialist help and guidance	1	2	3	4	5
1.10.	keep up with advances in IT	1	2	3	4	5
1.11.	improve my teaching	1	2	3	4	5
1.12.	improve my personal use of computers	1	2	3	4	5

1.13. **Please describe any other advantages you have experienced as a result of your membership of ACITT:** ______________________________

____

1.14 – 1.22. Please indicate the extent to which you value the various services and opportunities offered by ACITT:

		Low value				High value	Don't know
1.14.	Conferences	1	2	3	4	5	
1.15.	New hardware information	1	2	3	4	5	
1.16.	New software information	1	2	3	4	5	
1.17.	Product trials	1	2	3	4	5	
1.18.	Specialist help	1	2	3	4	5	
1.19.	Interaction with other professionals	1	2	3	4	5	
1.20.	Audience to which I can voice my opinions	1	2	3	4	5	
1.21.	Increased ICT skills	1	2	3	4	5	
1.22.	Ideas and help for funding for ICT projects	1	2	3	4	5	

1.23. Please indicate which of the following you consider to have limited the usefulness of the help you have received:

Time	
Resources	
The support cover requirement	
Travelling costs	
Other (please specify)	

1.24. What other services/support would you like to receive from ACITT?

____

____

1.25. Please indicate for how long you wish to remain an active member of ACITT:

Less than a year	
1-2 years	
2-5 years	
5-10 years	
More than 10 years	

Thank you for your time and help with our research.